51 GREATEST
MODERN
HEROES

51 GREATEST
MODERN
HEROES

HEROES WHO CHANGED THE WORLD

LUCAS OTTO

JAICO PUBLISHING HOUSE
Ahmedabad Bangalore Bhopal Chennai
Delhi Hyderabad Kolkata Lucknow Mumbai

Published by Jaico Publishing House
A-2 Jash Chambers, 7-A Sir Phirozshah Mehta Road
Fort, Mumbai - 400 001
jaicopub@jaicobooks.com
www.jaicobooks.com

© Encouragement Press, LLC

Published in arrangement with
Encouragement Press, LLC
1261 West Glenlake
Chicago, IL 60660

51 GREATEST MODERN HEROES
ISBN 978-81-8495-039-7

Authorized Reprint Edition for sale in the Indian Sub-Continent only
(India, Pakistan, Bangladesh, Sri Lanka and Nepal)

First Jaico Impression: 2009
Fourth Jaico Impression: 2011

Printed by
Pashupati Printers (P) Ltd., Delhi-95

Dedicated to orthopedic surgeon

Steven Haddad, M.D.

who is our hero for giving people their lives back.

About the Author

Lucas Otto, JD, is a writer, researcher, lawyer and consultant. He has been writing biographies of famous jurists and politicians for years, using much of his material on Websites and blogs. He has taken his experience and expanded it to include entertainers, church leaders, generals and civil rights leaders, among many groups represented. Otto put together a team of researchers and opinion makers and used this group to build his list of modern heroes.

Acknowledgements

Special thanks…and cheers to the following:

Luciano Ward

Table of Contents

Introduction

Everyone needs a hero. Heroes are people who make the news and are larger than life. They are the men and women of action, who think great thoughts, have nerves of steel or who make personal sacrifices–who prompt generations upon generations to speak of them in that very special way. We hold up heroes as models for our children–models of what we want them to be like and how we want them to act.

A modern hero is not always a great general or statesman (although there are some of them in our contemporary pantheon), but more often men and women who have influenced society, changed its views, sought to make the world a better place, entertained us or made us laugh or, even, given their lives for their ideals and their values. Our heroes are men and women from all walks of life, from all around the world, who through science, politics, war, letters, music, sports or the media stood head and shoulders above the rest of us. Heroes speak to us, sometimes directly but often indirectly, of the things that are most important in our own lives, and they challenge us to be like them, to follow them, to act like them and ultimately to respect them–even if we do not always agree with them.

Many of the heroes in this book are household names, recognized immediately for their presence on the world stage and for their accomplishments. But some of our heroes are not household names–9/11 victims and survivors and the veterans of World War II, for example. Some are from earlier generations, but without them, the lives that our generation has lived would have been significantly different. Some heroes are not people at all, but animated figures from comic books or characters from television and the movies.

Whatever you think a hero is, it is my hope that you will find this collection fun, entertaining and interesting. I also hope that one or two of these profiles will make you think about someone you thought you knew well in a new way. Or maybe one of these profiles will inspire you to take some actions to develop a great idea of your own. Every effort has been made to make the people real, showing both their admirable and less flattering sides. Even though they are our heroes, they are often not without controversy. After all, this is not a book about saints, but real people and real events.

Enjoy our heroes for what they are, learn from them, be inspired by them and most of all appreciate them for their contributions and their courage.

Happy reading!

Lucas Otto

plus one

9/11 Heroes,
Just Good People

Who They Are

As the fifth anniversary of the 9/11 disaster has come and gone, and the praise and memorials to all the victims have faded just a bit, we can only think of the thousands of people involved in this series of disasters as the truest of true heroes of the 21st century. Greatness has abounded throughout the world in the last 50 or 60 years, but nothing is more remarkable than the acts of self-sacrifice in an airplane or the willingness to go back into burning and falling buildings to save others.

This heroism has been recorded for posterity and as we move from that time, more books and movies will come forth to describe in graphic detail the lives and misfortunes of both victims and first-line responders. A nation will never forget the debt that it owes to so many people.

Stepping aside from the politics and the Monday morning recriminations about who should have known what, the events and people of 9/11 show the true spirit of human compassion and decency. Victims, survivors, helpers and those who cleaned up afterward are the truest of true heroes. We salute them all.

What Made Them

September 11, 2001, is one of those days on which people remember where they were and what they were doing when suddenly the world changed forever. In the midst of horrifying death and chaos, many of these people distinguished themselves and their country by risking their lives to save others.

They are all heroes in every sense of the word.

It was a perfect morning along the East Coast of the United States, but it would not last. Hijackers associated with Osama bin Laden and the al-Qaida terrorist group had boarded four airliners and were preparing to use them as guided missiles to destroy targets on American soil. Airport security was spotty in those days; the airplanes were not fully booked and all the flights were going to California–ensuring the maximum amount of damage from full loads of airplane fuel.

Three of the planes took off at approximately the same time. Soon after they were airborne, the hijackers made their moves, overpowering the flight crews with small knives that they had smuggled on board and threatening to blow up the plane with a bomb if the passengers did not cooperate. At least one hijacker per plane had received enough flight training to fly the airliner but not to land it (which, it would turn out, would not be necessary). The hijackers turned off the planes' transponders and began seeking their targets.

American Airlines Flight 11 struck the north face of the North Tower of the World Trade Center in New York at 8:46 a.m. Eastern time. At the time, the authorities and the media thought it was an accident. That view changed when a second airliner, United Airlines Flight 175, hit the South Tower of the World Trade Center only 15 minutes later. American Airlines Flight 77 crashed into the west wall of the Pentagon in Washington, D.C., at 9:37 a.m. Finally, the fourth plane, United Flight 93, crashed into an empty field in Somerset County, Pennsylvania, at 10:03 a.m.

The planes hit the upper floors of the World Trade Center towers, effectively dooming almost everyone above the crash zone. Victims below the crash zone faced fire, heavy smoke, nonfunctioning communications and blocked stairwells when trying to escape the buildings. Many of them helped free other people and were able to locate passable stairwells.

While the victims were trying to make their way down, members of the New York City fire department, police department and Port Authority were climbing the towers to try to rescue any survivors. In many places, the victims and the rescuers passed each other on the stairwells. Many of the rescuers who survived believed they would not be able to save many victims, but were willing to risk their lives for anyone who might still be alive.

The rescuers would soon find themselves fleeing along with the victims. A half-hour from the time it was struck by the airliner, the South Tower collapsed from the damage caused by the crash. Victims and rescuers in the North Tower could hear and feel the collapse and realized they needed to escape while they still could. The rescuers were ordered to return to the ground, but several lingered trying to find any victims that could make it downstairs. Thirty minutes after the

South Tower collapsed, the North Tower fell, killing or trapping anyone left in the structure, as well as heavily damaging nearby buildings. Even though some victims and rescuers were recovered by search teams who risked their lives going over the still unstable rubble, overall, 2,800 people were dead or missing, including fire fighters and police officers and everyone onboard the airliners.

At the same time rescuers, both inside and outside the damaged Pentagon, were trying to pull people out of the flames and smoke of the collapsed portion of the building. Professional firefighters took over the rescue operations, but not after many people were safely removed from the building by their co-workers. The collapsed section of the building claimed 189 lives, including all of the passengers and crew of the airliner.

Meanwhile, the final act of the tragedy was taking place in the skies over Pennsylvania. United Flight 93 would have been the fourth airliner to be guided into a target, but, due to heavy traffic, did not depart Newark International Airport until almost 45 minutes past its scheduled time. The plane was bound for San Francisco, California.

This delayed the takeover of the airliner by the hijackers to the point where news of the World Trade Center and Pentagon attacks was making its impact. Flight controllers sent out a warning to all flights to beware of cockpit intrusion. The pilot of Flight 93 tried to confirm the message when controllers suddenly heard the sounds of a fight and screams from the cockpit. After a few minutes, an Arabic-sounding voice told passengers to remain calm, there was a bomb on board and they were returning to the airport. In reality, the plane was making a slow turn to the south and east to get to its intended target, believed to have been the U.S. Capitol in Washington.

Two hijackers remained at the front of the plane and herded the passengers and remaining flight crew to the back. Passengers now had an opportunity to use cell phones to call family and friends and realized what their probable fate was going to be. Several of the passengers now started making plans to attempt to retake the plane. Many of them were larger than the hijackers and were even trained in martial arts. It is believed they discussed using a serving cart as a shield and improvised weapons, including carafes of boiling water.

The passengers made their move on the hijackers, forcing the two left in the cabin to retreat into the cockpit. Later, the recovered black box voice recorder would show the hijackers discussing whether to fight back or crash the airplane. Just when it sounded like the passengers were breaking through the cockpit door, one of the hijackers yelled, "Allahu akbar" (God is Great) and the recording cuts out.

The plane dove straight into the ground, impacting at almost 600 miles per hour and creating a crater 115 feet deep. The only remains of the plane were small bits of debris scattered around the area. None of the passengers survived.

America changed forever after September 11, 2001. All planes were grounded for several days, the military was instructed to shoot down any unauthorized air flights and the economy took a hard hit. The United States would eventually strike back by overthrowing the Taliban regime (believed to have aided al-Qaida) in Afghanistan and invading Iraq. Many American heroes have come from these battles, but it should never be forgotten that the first heroes of 9/11 were ordinary men and women who rose to the occasion under extraordinary danger.

The Legacy of the 9/11 Heroes

The sacrifice of the heroes of 9/11 was an inspiration to a country in a state of shock. Their bravery showed that whether a trained professional or an average person, Americans were willing to put their lives on the line to help others in danger.

The country has expressed its debt of gratitude to the 9/11 victims, rescuers and passengers of United Flight 93. Memorials to the heroes include the Flight 93 Memorial in Shanksville, Pennsylvania, and the soon-to-be-completed Pentagon memorial.

As upsetting and devastating as the actual day of September 11th, the trauma and confusion continue more than five years after the event as the city and people of New York (as well as the rest of the country) struggle with what should be done to the site of the World Trade Center as a memorial to the victims. At the same time, the Port Authority of New York and New Jersey, which owns the land and the buildings of the entire World Trade Center complex (recall that there are more than just the two major towers), wants to replace the lost buildings with a complex that is both sensitive and economically viable.

In addition, the families of the victims (many of whom were never recovered from the rubble for proper burial) have equally strong opinions as to whether the site has been cleared of human remains. (As late as 2006, new efforts were made to recover victims.) To say the least, the tension and disagreements as to what the future will hold both for rebuilding and for a permanent memorial are fever-pitch. Everyone has a view on the matter.

The Lower Manhattan Development Corporation (LMDC) began a world-wide competition to design the World Trade Center Memorial in April of 2003. It would turn out to be one of the largest public design contests ever, generating competing ideas from all 50 states and 93 countries. By January of 2004, LMDC's selection committee had chosen the entry by Michael Arad and Peter Walker, Reflecting Absence, as the winning bid. The design includes two large recessed pools of water (the original footprint of the twin towers); the pools will be about 30 feet below ground level. On street level will be a park with informal and formal groupings of trees.

The names of the victims in the memorial will be displayed in front of a curtain of water. Once again controversy arose as to what order the names were to be listed and how they were to be listed. An underground passageway will lead to an alcove where memorials can take place; included will be a large stone container to hold all the unidentified remains of victims. A Tribute of Light was the first, permanent feature put in place as a memorial. Not only the memorial itself but the costs associated with the project have come under a great deal of criticism— one estimate makes it as high as $1 billion, a figure rejected by the mayor of New York and others involved in raising the staggering sums needed to build the memorial.

In addition to the memorial, a series of new buildings is planned for the site—four commercial buildings and one residential building are shown in the final designs. (Assuming anything about this reconstruction project can ever be final with ongoing disputes by the public, the governor, the developer and architects on what the area should look like.) Work has begun on the first building, World Trade Center Tower 1 or, more familiarly, the Freedom Tower. The height of the building is estimated to be over 1,300 feet, although the final number is not confirmed and may not be until much later in construction. The cost of this one building alone is estimated at $2.6 billion, with the State of New York one of the largest tenants in the building, possibly occupying as much as one million square feet.

The Resources

Recent films on the events of 9/11 include *United 93* and *World Trade Center*. There have been many documentaries and made-for-television films on what happened that day, almost all available on video. You can find a variety of information by visiting *www.september11news.com.*

Many books have been written about the fateful day and the story of the heroes, including *The 9/11 Commission Report,* W.W. Norton, 2004; *The Puzzle of 9/11,* BookSurge Publishing, 2005; *The September 11 Photo Project,* Regan Books, 2002; *September 11: An Oral History,* Doubleday, 2002; and *One Nation: America Remembers September 11, 2001,* Little, Brown, 2001.

Muhammad Ali,
Boxer

Who He Is

In 1999, *Sports Illustrated* named Muhammad Ali Sportsman of the Century. Not Boxer of the Century. Sportsman of the Century. Not of the year. Not even of the decade. Of the century. He needs no further introduction. He is one of the greatest sports heroes in history. Period.

But it is not just because of these accolades that Ali is one of our heroes. In and out of the ring, he was our superhero: bold, confident, abrasive, opinionated, a man of conviction and a model for children and adults everywhere. There were times when we loved to hate him, but always we admired and respected him.

What Made the Man

Cassius Marcellus Clay Jr. was born on January 17, 1942, in Louisville, Kentucky to Odessa Grady Clay and Cassius Marcellus Clay Sr. His love affair with boxing began when he was 12 years old. His bicycle was stolen from in front of a department store. A very upset young Clay found a policeman, Joe Elsby Martin, Sr., coach of the Louisville city boxing program. Clay told Martin what had happened and that he wanted to whup whoever had stolen his bike. Martin was quick to respond that Clay should learn to fight if he really intended to whup someone. The 89-pound boy showed up at Louisville's Columbia Gym the very next day.

He started taking boxing lessons from Martin, who taught him the moves that would someday lead to his famous saying, "Float like a butterfly, sting like a bee."

From that fateful day in 1954, Clay approached boxing with a more determined and committed attitude than most of the other young fighters. He was victorious in 100 out of 108 matches during his amateur career, winning six Kentucky Golden Gloves championships, two National Golden Gloves championships and two

National Amateur Athletic Union titles before he reached the age of 18. He also took home a light heavyweight gold medal from the 1960 Olympics in Rome, just a few months after he turned 18.

Throughout his professional boxing career, Clay never lost his sass. He was always running his mouth and was dubbed The Louisville Lip. Not only did he constantly dog his opponents, but he also spoke in front of the media, which was rare in the days when managers usually talked on behalf of their fighters. Clay's big mouth certainly threw some fighters off their game, as did his unorthodox heavyweight boxing style of relying on his reflexes and footwork rather than his hands to protect himself from getting hit in the face.

Clay's distinctive and unusual style of fighting would eventually lead him to become one of the best, if not the best, heavyweight boxers of all time. He won his first professional fight on October 29, 1960, in Louisville, and, from 1960 to 1963, his record was 19-0, with 15 knockouts. In 1964, Clay was the No. 1 contender for Sonny Liston's title. He beat Liston in the seventh round and shocked the world even further by announcing the next day that he had joined the Nation of Islam and changed his name to Cassius X. Soon after, Elijah Muhammad, the leader of the Nation, gave Clay his true Islamic name: Muhammad Ali.

That same year, Ali failed the qualifying exam for the Armed Forces. But he was reclassified 1A in early 1966 when the exam was revised. However, as a result of his beliefs in the Quran, which teaches against fighting in Christian wars, Ali refused to serve in the army during the Vietnam War. He was pretty much banned from boxing in the United States and could only accept fights in other countries for almost all of 1966.

After defending his title against Liston, whom he knocked out in the seventh round, on May 25, 1965, in Lewiston, Maine, and then defeating former champion Floyd Patterson in November of that same year, Ali defended his title another eight times. The force that eventually stopped him was not another fighter, but rather the Professional Boxing Commission, which took the championship title away from him near the end of 1967 because of his refusal to be drafted for the Vietnam War. The commission refused to let him fight professionally for more than 3 years, during which time Ali earned wages by speaking at rallies on college campuses that were against the war.

Eventually regaining his boxing license, Ali fought his first match against the undefeated champion, Joe Frazier, on March 8, 1971, at Madison Square Garden. The fight was coined The Fight of the Century or, more simply, The Fight. Frazier beat him in points, knocking him down with a hard left hook in the last round.

However, a few years later, Ali beat Frazier in points at their 1974 rematch. He was on his way to another shot at the title.

This shot, The Rumble in the Jungle, would prove to be the most important one of Ali's career. The fight was against George Foreman and was one of the first matches to be promoted by Don King. It was set for October 30, 1974, in Kinshasa, Zaire. Ali beat Foreman by a knockout in the eighth round to regain the championship title.

In 1975, Ali converted from the Nation of Islam to orthodox Sunni Islam and won what many of his fans felt should have been his last fight before retirement. He fought Joe Frazier on October 1 in Quezon City, Philippines, and won by a technical knockout after 14 rounds, when Frazier's trainer refused to let him continue fighting. The fight, coined The Thrilla in Manila, became the fifth Ali match to be named Fight of the Year by Ring Magazine.

Ali finally retired permanently after he lost a 10-round unanimous decision to Trevor Berbick on December 11, 1980, in the Bahamas. He left the world of professional boxing with a career record of 56 wins (37 by knockout) and 5 losses.

The Legacy of the Man

After Ali's retirement, he was diagnosed with Parkinson's syndrome in the early 1980s. Doctors argued about whether or not his symptoms had been caused by boxing and he was finally diagnosed with Pugilistic Parkinson's syndrome, a variation of the disease that plagues professional boxers due to receiving multiple blows to the head.

Ali has managed to accomplish much since stepping out of the boxing ring. In practicing his Islamic duty of carrying out good deeds, he has donated millions of dollars to organizations and disadvantaged people of all religious denominations. He has also been involved in work that is political and moral at the same time. He went to Iraq in 1990 to meet with Saddam Hussein and was able to negotiate the release of 15 hostages. He also asked the U.S. government and its people to come to the aid of the refugees in Rwanda. It has been estimated that Ali has helped to feed more than 22 million people who are afflicted by hunger.

On November 19, 2005, the doors of the $60 million nonprofit Muhammad Ali Center opened in downtown Louisville. The center not only showcases Ali's boxing memorabilia but also promotes the themes of peace, respect, social responsibility and personal growth. In addition, he has received the following awards:

- Ellis Island Medal of Honor (1986)
- United Nations Messenger of Peace Award (1998)
- BBC Sports Personality of the Century Award (1999)
- Living Legend Award, Library of Congress (2000)
- Presidential Medal of Freedom (2005)

Ali has also written an autobiography, called *The Greatest*, and tried his hand at acting when the book was adapted into a film. He received positive reviews for his work in the movie. He has been married four times and has seven daughters and two sons. He currently resides at a small farm in Michigan with his wife, Yolanda "Lonnie" Ali.

Amongst all his activities, boxing has always remained an important part of Ali's life. According to the documentary *When We Were Kings*, when asked about whether he had regrets about boxing because of the disorder he developed, Ali said that if he had not become a boxer, he would still be a painter in Louisville. But Muhammad Ali remains a boxer at heart, and he will remain in the hearts of others throughout the world long after he is gone.

The Resources

For a deeper look inside the life of the man who called himself The Greatest, make sure to read his daughter's first book, *More Than a Hero: Muhammad Ali's Life Lessons Presented Through His Daughter's Eyes*, Atria, 2000.

Lance Edward Armstrong, *Cyclist*

Who He Is

Lance Armstrong is an American who achieved the longest-ever string of victories in the Tour de France–a European (read French) sporting event. Further, he became a world hero not just for his athletic supremacy, but because he overcame cancer and still managed to maintain his supremacy in an enormously competitive and grueling sport.

Naturally, heroes are haunted with rumors and innuendos–in this case, about whether Armstrong ever used performance-enhancing drugs. No one, the critics said, could be this good and this successful without something on the side to help his performance. To date, nothing has been proved, but the rumors continue to dent his reputation.

However, as a cancer survivor, he is an indisputable hero, continuing to drive home the importance of early detection of cancer and the need for a cure. He is the poster child of survivors and inspires millions who are victims of the disease.

What Made the Man

He was born on September 17, 1971, in Plano, Texas, where he was raised by his mother (his father left the family soon after Lance's birth). Armstrong developed an interest in being a triathlete and developed his own training regimen by riding his bike while anchored in a pool.

By age 13, he was competing regularly in triathlons, but it soon became clear that his talent and interest centered on cycling. It was during this time that Armstrong demonstrated his single-minded devotion to succeed. His success as an amateur and his obvious talent as a cyclist led to the Junior National Cycling Team inviting Armstrong to train with them. He petitioned his high school to allow him to take 42 days off from school during the final semester of his senior year to take part in the training. The school refused, so Armstrong simply left school and started training with the team.

Armstrong continued to compete as an amateur and won the U.S. Amateur Championships in 1991 and finished fourteenth in the Olympics road race. Armstrong believed that this success indicated cycling was the sport for him, and he turned professional in 1992. He started inauspiciously by finishing last in his first pro race, the Classica San Sebastian—the only time that Armstrong would finish that far back in a professional race.

He earned his first major professional victory the next year by winning the World Cycling Championship in Oslo, Norway. The king of Norway invited Armstrong to an audience, based on his impressive performance. Armstrong would only appear if the invitation included his mother. The king quickly agreed.

After tasting his first professional victory, Armstrong turned his attention to the prestigious Tour de France. He joined Team Motorola and won stages in the 1993 and 1995 races. At this time, he also won several individual races, including the 1992 and 1996 Tour du Pont, considered the United States' premier cycling race.

Armstrong briefly left the pro tour to take part in the 1996 Olympics, but was disappointed in his nonmedal performance. This perceived failure acted as an impetus, and he began training even harder with his eyes set now on the Tour de France.

However, this commitment to athletic success was shaken severely when, in October 1996, Armstrong was diagnosed with stage three testicular cancer. The cancer had metastasized and was spreading to his lungs and brain. Armstrong was given only a 40 percent chance of survival, but like his racing, he viewed his cancer as a challenge. His right testicle and a brain lesion were removed, and he received extensive chemotherapy. Armstrong recovered from the disease (his doctors would tell him later that his actual chances had been much smaller than 40 percent).

Even during his recovery, he kept his mind on racing and insisted on using a more radical form of chemotherapy that would have less long-term debilitating effects on his breathing.

Armstrong resumed training to race, but had been dropped by his team during his bout with cancer. In 1998, he joined the then-new U.S. Postal Service cycling team and quickly returned to form. He was now poised to make racing history by returning to the Tour de France.

One of the more ironic side effects in Armstrong's chemotherapy is that the treatment caused some loss of muscle mass in his upper body. This proved to be a benefit to his racing, giving him more stamina in the grueling mountain portions of the Tour de France.

Armstrong won his first Tour de France in 1999. He would go on to win for the next 6 years, making him the only cyclist to win seven Tour de France races. What was even more remarkable is that in all but two of these races his lead-time was 6 minutes or more ahead of the second place finisher. In 2005, he won his last Tour de France, as a member of the Discovery Channel Pro Cycling Team.

Armstrong's seven consecutive Tour de France victories rank as one of the greatest sporting achievements in history. Many racers and cycling enthusiasts have tried to explain his success: He focused mainly on the Tour de France (some criticized him for ignoring other racing events); he trained almost all year on the same type of terrain as that offered by the Tour de France; his mental preparation and strategy planning for the race were just as intense as his physical training; his unusual aerobic stamina allowed him to maintain a higher cadence at a lower gear on his bicycle; and he improved the cooperation between his sponsors, suppliers and cycling team.

A controversial aspect of Armstrong's success is the recurring allegations that he used performance-enhancing drugs. These allegations surfaced in a book, *L.A. Confidential: Les Secrets de Lance Armstrong,* which quoted fellow riders saying that they and Armstrong had used such drugs. Sections of the book appeared in the British newspaper, The Sunday Times; Armstrong sued for libel and the case was settled out of court with the newspaper printing an apology.

In 2005, the French sports newspaper, L'Equipe, printed that Armstrong had been using drugs since 1999. In 2006, the French newspaper, Le Monde, reported claims that Armstrong had been using performance-enhancing drugs based on a deposition taken as part of a lawsuit that Armstrong filed against SCA Promotions. Later the same year, The Los Angeles Times reviewed the facts of the SCA trial and also other allegations against Armstrong.

These later reports were unimportant, because in 2005, after investigations by cycling authorities into the questionable drug-testing methodology of LNDD, the French national anti-doping laboratory, Armstrong was exonerated of illegal drug use based on the improper handling and testing of athletes' urine samples.

During this period, Armstrong and Kristin, his wife of 6 years, filed for divorce in 2005. It was revealed that Armstrong had developed a relationship with rock star

Sheryl Crow in 2003. The news of their relationship was made public in 2005, but the couple split in 2006.

Armstrong retired from competitive racing after his seventh Tour de France victory in 2005. He remains active in promoting cycling, cancer awareness and physical fitness. His achievements expanded American awareness of the Tour de France and helped make the race an even more high-profile international sporting event.

The Legacy of the Man

Lance Armstrong will always be remembered as one of the greatest athletes of all time, but his reputation may always have a cloud over it because of the drug-use allegations. Armstrong continues to defend himself in public and on his Website.

Armstrong remains an advocate for cancer awareness and early treatment of the disease. He sits on the President's Anti-Cancer Panel, and founded the Lance Armstrong Foundation for fighting cancer. One of its fundraising methods was to sell rubber band Livestrong bracelets. The bracelets became very popular during the 2005 Tour de France.

There have also been rumors that Armstrong may enter politics in his native Texas. Lately, he has been making statements that sound like he might be open to eventually running for office.

The Resources

You can find almost all you want to know about Lance Armstrong, including daily postings from him, on his Website at *www.lancearmstrong.com* or from the Lance Armstrong Foundation at *www.livestrong.org*.

You can read about Armstrong in his autobiographies, *It's Not About the Bike: My Journey Back to Life,* Berkeley Trade, 2001, and *Every Second Counts*, Broadway, 2004; *Lance Armstrong's War*, Harper Press, 2006; *23 Days in France: Inside Lance Armstrong's Record-Breaking Tour de France Victory*, De Capo Press, 2005; and *No Mountain High Enough: Raising Lance Raising Me*, Broadway, 2005.

3

Neil Alden Armstrong, *Astronaut*

Who He Is

Heroes are often the stuff of firsts–to navigate around the world, to fly across the Atlantic, to climb Mt. Everest and dozens more. Certainly any individual with the courage to land on the moon with what could be described, at best, as very tentative technology and planning, has to be one of our heroes.

The wonder of Neil Armstrong is the complete lack of ego and ambition beyond his desire to be part of the NASA mission and program. Whether active or retired, he accepted the admiration of millions with the humility of a child. His right kind of stuff can hardly be underestimated, and his superior intellectual ability helped NASA with an ambitious and politically sensitive mission to the moon.

How does history understand this seemingly aloof man? Gently, kindly and with a great deal of affection and appreciation, the nation has chosen to honor a truly modest hero who seemingly does not wish to be honored or lauded.

What Made the Man

Neil Armstrong was the first man to walk on the moon, and the phrase he uttered when he first stepped foot on the surface of Tranquility Base has become part of the English folklore. What many people do not know is that Armstrong, unlike most of his fellow astronauts, was a civilian and not part of the military.

Armstrong is from America's heartland, born on August 5, 1930, in his home at Wapakoneta, Ohio. His father was an Ohio government employee and the family moved frequently during Armstrong's childhood. Popular history has Armstrong taking his first plane ride at age six, where he reportedly fell in love with aviation. By the time he was 15, he was saving his money to take flying lessons and progressed rapidly in a number of aircraft to get his pilot's license.

Armstrong attended Purdue University. His education was funded by a national program that required him to commit to 3 years of military service after 2 years of academic study, then finishing the final 2 years after his release from active duty. He was called up to naval service in 1949 and, after jet training, began flying combat missions in the Korean War. During one mission, his plane was badly mauled by anti-aircraft fire. He was forced to eject and, as luck would have it, was picked up by a roommate from flight school.

After flying 78 missions in Korea and receiving several commendations, he left the Navy in 1952 and returned to Purdue University to complete his degree in aeronautical engineering.

He met his first wife, Janet Elizabeth Shearon, after he returned to Purdue. The two married in 1956. Armstrong, who had been applying repeatedly to be a test pilot and research pilot, was finally accepted and was stationed at Edwards Air Force Base in California. He and Janet settled into the area and, during this period, the couple had three children, one of whom died at an early age from brain cancer.

In 1957, Armstrong made his first flight in a rocket plane, thought at the time to be the natural transition to real spacecraft. He would end up flying the Bell X-1B and the North American X-15. He had the usual mishaps for a test pilot, but managed to walk away from all of them. Most of his fellow test pilots valued his engineering ability and one said that "he had a mind that absorbed things like a sponge." Other old-guard pilots, such as Chuck Yeager, thought that the engineers approached flying too mechanically and that they got into trouble because they did not have a real feel for flying.

As Armstrong was coming to the end of his test pilot career, the United States was caught up in the race with the USSR to be the first to land a man on the moon and return safely. The Mercury program was already sending up astronauts in solo flights and NASA was now planning the next phase with two astronauts flying on Gemini flights.

Armstrong would later say he had no moment of revelation that he wanted to be an astronaut. When word came out that NASA was accepting applications for the Gemini astronauts, his interest increased and he applied for what was called the new nine. He was accepted into the program as a civilian and spent his first 2 years as an astronaut on the ground undergoing extensive, grueling physical and mental training. During this time, Armstrong used his engineering background to improve the NASA flight simulators, developing techniques and software that are still being used.

Armstrong was named command pilot for Gemini 8, with David Scott as pilot. The flight was the most ambitious ever attempted and would involve the Gemini spacecraft docking with an unmanned Agena Target Vehicle (a crucial maneuver necessary for the missions to the moon). The spacecraft successfully docked with the Agena, but soon afterwards both ships started rocking uncontrollably. The roll increased after NASA directed the vehicles to undock and, if left unchecked, would have caused the astronauts to black out. The crew used the reentry control system to stop the roll, but that caused the ship to return earlier than planned, canceling other activities, including a spacewalk for Scott.

Astronaut opinion was divided on whether Armstrong had made mistakes that caused the near disaster, but NASA later admitted that errors in planning and training were behind the problems.

By now Gemini was almost over and the Apollo program was starting. Following orbital flights of the three-person Apollo spacecraft and two trips to the moon (one to test the Lunar Excursion Module in space), NASA was ready to attempt a landing with Apollo 11. Armstrong was made commander of the spacecraft, and, after deciding Armstrong had a more matter-of-fact personality, NASA named him to be the first man to walk on the moon. Apollo 11 blasted off on July 17, 1969, with Armstrong, lunar module pilot Buzz Aldrin and command module pilot Michael Armstrong.

Apollo 11 landed on the moon on July 20. A few hours after landing, Armstrong descended the LEM ladder to the lunar surface and said, "That's one small step for a man, one giant leap for mankind." Radio static masked the "a" from the first part of the statement, although Armstrong admitted later he sometimes omitted syllables when he spoke. He said he had come up with the statement only while waiting to leave the LEM for the moon.

After his triumphant return, Armstrong announced he would not fly in space anymore. He resigned from NASA and accepted an engineering teaching position at the University of Cincinnati. He avoided exploiting his achievements and generally kept a very low profile, repeatedly refusing any efforts to get him into politics. His frequent absences had taken a toll on his marriage, and wife his divorced him in 1989. He married Carol Held Knight in 1994. He continues to teach and consult with NASA.

The Legacy of the Man

Neil Armstrong was the perfect man in the perfect place at the perfect time. His no-nonsense approach to life and his work stood in stark contrast to the drama of walking on the moon and made the event even more exciting. He will go down in history, along with people like Charles Lindbergh, as a man who defined an era.

Still, that same style led to a certain distancing between Armstrong and the American people, helped along by his perceptions of the misuse of his name and of his statement when he landed on the moon.

No matter what, Armstrong summed up what Meriwether Lewis called undaunted courage in traveling on an incredibly dangerous mission with the whole world watching. He reportedly is looking forward to the United States returning to the moon and eventually landing people on Mars.

The Resources

There have been dozens of documentaries and fictional films involving the Apollo program and the first moon landing. One of the better ones is *Apollo 11: Men on the Moon*, from Spacecraft Films, 2003. NASA also has extensive information on Armstrong and his Gemini and Apollo missions at *www.nasa.gov.*

Armstrong's authorized biography is *First Man: The Life of Neil A. Armstrong*, Simon and Schuster, 2005. Other books on Armstrong include *First on the Moon*, William Konecky Associates, 2002; *One Giant Leap: The Story of Neil Armstrong*, Houghton Mifflin, 2001; and *One Giant Leap: Neil Armstrong's Stellar American Journey*, Forge Books, 2004.

Lucille Desiree Ball, *Comedian*

Who She Is

Imagine our hero, not as a great thinker, statesman or author, but as an absolutely zany woman with wacky ideas, putting herself and her friend, Ethel, in ridiculous situations, and having the entire nation love her for it!

She is our hero because she made us laugh louder and longer than anyone on television. She is great because she was an astute businesswoman who built a prominent production company–and you thought Oprah was the first!

When you think of genius, of greatness, remember Lucy stuffing candy into her uniform on the assembly line or advertising a mineral supplement (getting increasingly drunk with each retake of the commercial) or stomping grapes at a vineyard.

What Made the Woman

Despite her public image as a screwball, Lucille Ball was a shrewd performer who knew exactly what she wanted. She was a successful producer who, along with husband Desi Arnaz, formed Desilu Productions, one of the most profitable independent production companies in Hollywood history.

However, it was a long and often frustrating journey that led to the fame and notoriety that her comic skills merited. Ball was born on August 6, 1911, in Jamestown, New York, to Henry Durrell Ball and Desieree DeDe Eve Hunt. She was always proud of her family background, which traced itself back to the earliest American colonists (through her father's side, she was related to George Washington).

Ball's father's job as a telephone lineman sent the family to live all over the country. Henry Ball died in 1915 from typhoid fever and Ball and her brother Fred were raised by her working mother and grandparents. Her grandfather loved the theater and took the family to vaudeville shows. He saw how much the girl enjoyed them and encouraged her to get into performing.

During this period, Ball developed her reputation as a hard worker, helping to support the family while still finding time to perform in plays for the local Elks Club and her high school. She even staged her own production of Charley's Aunt, Encouraged by her experiences and her grandfather, Ball, in 1926, enrolled at the John Murray Anderson American Academy of Dramatic Art in Manhattan.

She was counseled not to continue with her acting career because of what her teachers perceived as a terminal case of shyness.

Ball persevered in her dream by returning to New York and getting intermittent work as a chorus girl and model (at one point, she was the Chesterfield cigarette girl). After suffering a series of hirings and firings on Broadway, she got an uncredited role as one of the Goldwyn girls for movie producer Samuel Goldwyn. This led to her going out to Hollywood, where her first picture was *Roman Scandals*, co-starring Eddie Cantor.

Ball never made a big splash in the movies. She worked steadily in her early years at RKO Radio and Columbia Pictures, appearing with the Marx Brothers and The Three Stooges. By 1938, she was achieving star billing in movies, but these were mostly B-films. In some cases, Ball was cast in the role only because an actress with a larger reputation did not want to play it. After RKO, she worked briefly at MGM studios (where she was dubbed the Technicolor girl because of her red hair and bright smile) then returned to RKO where it seemed her movie career might be finished.

While she was trying to establish herself as a movie actress, Ball fell in love with Cuban bandleader and actor Desi Arnaz. The two worked together in 1940 on the musical *Two Many Girls* and eloped soon after the film was over. Almost from the beginning, the marriage was troubled, with Arnaz openly unfaithful. The two separated and filed for divorce in 1944. However, before the divorce became final, Ball and Arnaz decided to give their marriage one more chance. Ball was now convinced that the best way to keep her husband from straying was to find projects they could both work on. Their first and only big project would revolutionize television comedy.

In 1948, Ball was cast as the wacky wife in the radio comedy *My Favorite Husband* for CBS. The show was a hit and the network approached Ball to make a television version. Ball refused unless Arnaz was cast as the husband in what would become *I Love Lucy*. The pilot did not impress the CBS executives, so Ball and Arnaz toured in a vaudeville act based on the premise of the show. The act was a big success and CBS decided to add the show to its schedule in 1951.

Besides being the first television show to star a real-life husband and wife (and to have them be ethnically mixed), *I Love Lucy* was a pioneer in several production techniques. The show was filmed in front of a live audience. Up to then, almost all television shows were broadcast live or recorded on Kinescope. Ball and Arnaz wanted *I Love Lucy* to be shot on the much cleaner medium of film.

Arnaz hired legendary cinematographer Karl Freund to come up with a new way to shoot a half-hour television show on film. Freund created the three-camera technique, using one camera to film long shots, one for medium shots and the other to shoot close-ups. This technique is still being used in most television comedies today.

Ball and Arnaz formed Desilu Productions to manage the production and promotion of the show. Arnaz found he was a talented manager and Ball quickly got up-to-speed about the business. In addition to *I Love Lucy,* Desilu would produce such hit comedies as *Make Room for Daddy, The Dick Van Dyke Show* and *The Andy Griffith Show*, as well as highly regarded drama series such as *The Untouchables, I Spy, Star Trek* and *Mission: Impossible.*

I Love Lucy was a tremendous hit in its run from 1951 through 1957. One example of the blending of fact and fiction involved Ball's pregnancy with her second child. Ball and Arnaz wanted to incorporate her real-life pregnancy into the show, but the network balked at showing a pregnant woman and even using the word pregnant. CBS finally relented on allowing Ball to appear pregnant, but the actors had to use the word expecting. The episode where she gave birth (coinciding with the real-life birth) is one of the highest-rated shows in television history.

From 1957 to 1960, the show morphed into *The Lucy-Desi Comedy Hour*, retaining the original cast but moving the characters to the country. By this time, Ball and Arnaz's marriage was over and after the show went off the air in 1960, the couple divorced. A year later, Ball remarried comedian Gary Morton. Morton joined Desilu as a producer and was soon running many aspects of the company.

After a brief stint on Broadway and appearances in a couple of films, Ball returned to television in the successful *The Lucy Show* and later *Here's Lucy*, which ran until 1974. Despite her reputation, Ball's career went nowhere fast after she left television. A film version of the musical *Mame* was a flop, and her attempt at returning to television also ended in failure.

Ball made only a few personal appearances during her last years. She died from a ruptured aorta following open-heart surgery on April 26, 1989.

The Legacy of the Woman

During her heyday on television, Lucille Ball was called the queen of comedy, and few would dispute it. Her shows were undeniably hilarious. She proved almost single-handedly that women could be just as funny as men.

Ball also broke the gender barrier for women on the business side of Hollywood. After her divorce from Arnaz, she ran Desilu Productions, later selling it to Gulf-Western for a very healthy profit.

This success was not without its price. Her marriage to Arnaz was never smooth. Her children said she was a cold and controlling mother who had few friends in show business. However, her audience cared little about this, and her lovable screwball in *I Love Lucy* is still seen every day on some television station or cable network.

The Resources

You can find several DVD compilations of *I Love Lucy, The Lucy Show* and *Here's Lucy*. Other information on Ball can be found on *www.lucilleball.com*.

Lucille Ball published an autobiography *Love, Lucy,* Berkeley, reissued 1997. Other books on Ball include *Lucille: The Life of Lucille Ball*, Watson-Guptill, 2001; *Ball of Fire: The Tumultuous Life and Comic Art of Lucille Ball*, Knopf, 2003; and *Desilu: The Story of Lucille Ball and Desi Arnaz*, Harper Paperbacks, 1994.

5

Barbara Millicent Roberts
"Barbie"
Toy Superstar

Who She Is

Can a toy be a hero? It can if it brings joy and entertainment to generations of girls. It can if it becomes a household name, an icon, a symbol of this, a symbol of that, a symbol of ... take your pick. And a toy is certainly a hero if, instead of referring to the toy as it, you feel more comfortable saying she. And she is Barbie.

She is a hero because she is a best friend, a companion, a confidante. She can be shared with others or played with alone. But most importantly, she is always there when needed–a reflection of ourselves and our times.

What Made the Doll

The Barbie doll is one of the most popular toys in history. From her creation in the late 1950s, there have been millions of the dolls and accessories sold. The toy is still much sought after by collectors and little girls of all ages and is a $1.9 billion a year industry. Mattel, which markets the doll, says that approximately three Barbie dolls are sold every second.

Mattel had very humble beginnings before the Barbie doll helped make it one of the most successful toy companies in the world. It was founded by Ruth and Elliot Handler. The company slowly grew into a more structured business and by the mid-1950s, the Handlers found themselves with less and less input in the creative side of the company.

Handler noticed that her daughter, Barbara, did not play with baby dolls. She preferred to play with dolls that were adults. Handler realized that there was a hole in the market, a hole that could be filled with an adult doll. She was excited about what she believed was a sure-fire success and took the idea to the executives who were now running Mattel. They quickly brushed aside Handler's adult doll idea as being impractical, and too expensive to create and market.

Handler was still convinced she had a great idea, but was unsure how to proceed. Finally, during a visit to Germany with her daughter, Barbara, Handler found in a German shop window a doll called the Bild Lilli. The doll, made to look like an adult, was the type of doll that Handler had in mind, and she bought three of them (one for her daughter and two to take back to the naysayers at Mattel).

Doing her research, Handler found out the Bild Lilli doll was based on a popular character that appeared in a comic strip for the German newspaper, Die Bild-Zeitung. The character was a society girl with a head for fashion. She knew what she wanted and was not above manipulating men to get it. Ironically, the doll was originally marketed in 1955 to men and was sold in tobacco shops. It eventually caught on with children, who dressed her in outfits that were sold separately (a brilliant marketing move that vastly increased profits). The doll became very popular and was exported overseas, including the United States.

Handler finally persuaded Mattel to let her change the doll and showcase it at various toy shows to gauge its popularity. She worked with engineer Jack Ryan to revamp the concept of the doll into what is still the basic design. She gave it the all-American name of Barbie after her daughter Barbara.

Barbie made her official debut at the New York International Toy Fair on March 9, 1959 (which is listed as Barbie's official birth date). Interest was immediately strong and Mattel finally realized they had a potential blockbuster on their hands. In 1964, to cement their hold on the market, they purchased the rights to the rival Bild Lilli doll and discontinued its manufacture.

The original Barbie dolls were either blonde or brunette and wore a zebra-striped swimsuit and signature topknot ponytail. Later Barbies would feature other hairstyles and hair colors. The genius of the marketing of the doll was to feature it as a teenage fashion model so that girls could be encouraged to build up a large wardrobe of clothing and accessories. Much of the early Barbie wardrobe was designed by Mattel fashion designer Charlotte Johnson, who took her inspiration from the New York and Paris fashion runways.

During the next few years, Mattel would introduce the Ken doll as her boyfriend and Skipper, her little sister doll. Other dolls would come and go from Barbie's circle. During the 1960s, the Mattel designers gave Barbie bendable legs (making it easier for owners to change her clothes) and a redesigned face that had Barbie look straight ahead at attention. She was also given the power of speech.

In 1980, Mattel stretched the political correctness
of the doll even more by creating Black Barbie and
Hispanic Barbie dolls.

Not only did Mattel make billions of dollars on sales of the actual dolls and clothing, the company also profited by the creation of Barbie cars, boats, workplaces and the famous Barbie Dream House. All these items were sold separately. Barbie also started to take on very different personas based on the type of occupation with which the individual doll was associated. Over the years, these occupations included astronaut, gymnast, rapper, soldier, doctor, paleontologist, rock star, firefighter, McDonald's employee and even a candidate for president.

Barbie, her friends, fashions and accessories quickly moved from being toys to being much-sought-after collectible items. Mattel has estimated there are over 100,000 avid collectors who buy as many as 20 Barbie dolls every year. The collectors created special terms for the merchandise they were purchasing and trading, including collector edition (designed for collectors 14 and older), customized (designed exclusively for specific retailers), limited edition (collector editions made in limited quantities), vintage and modern (dolls made before and after 1972, respectively) and OOAK (one-of-a-kind dolls that have been modified by an individual artist).

The doll has her own biography that identifies her as Barbara Millicent Roberts. She was born in Willows, Wisconsin, and attended Willows High School and Manhattan International High School in New York. Besides her friends, she has 38 known pets, including cats, dogs, horses, pandas, lion cubs and a zebra. Some of the world's top designers have created outfits for the doll. Barbie has also become a multimedia presence, featured in books, cartoon videos, music and video games.

The Legacy of the Doll

Fans of Barbie respond to criticism of how the doll represents life to a little girl by stressing the number and variety of occupations Barbie has done over the years. The critics believe that Barbie presents a type of body image that most girls will never achieve and could possibly lead to eating disorders. In addition, Barbie is seen as an example of Western materialism and is not popular in all countries of the world (especially in the Middle East).

Besides problems with the body image the doll presents, many critics have also pointed out that there is negative stereotyping associated with the doll–talking models that can only remark about going out and shopping for clothes. Mattel continued to respond to these critics and has recently widened the doll's waist and created more ethnically diverse versions.

Of course, anything as popular as Barbie was bound to create its own types of satire and parodies. A series of real-life Barbies were released with such names as Trailer Trash Barbie. The character was the subject of the song *Barbie Girl* by the Danish pop-group Aqua, and has been lampooned on *Saturday Night Live* and *The Tonight Show*. The doll, renamed Malibu Stacy, is Lisa's favorite toy on *The Simpsons*.

Despite the critics' use of Barbie as a derogatory name for a shallow female, Barbie's future seems secure. She is now on her own, having separated from Ken in 2004 (supposedly because he would not marry her) and still occupies a special place both in the hearts of little girls and on the shelves of collectors.

The Resources

Mattel has created a variety of videos and books based on Barbie and her friends, all of which are easily available. There are a variety of Websites for Barbie fans of all ages with *www.barbiecollector.com* being a particularly popular site.

Books about Barbie include *The Ultimate Barbie Doll Book: Identification and Price Guide*, Krause Publications, 2004; *The Story of Barbie Doll*, Collector Books, 1999; *The Barbie Chronicles: A Living Doll Turns Forty*, Touchstone, 1999; and *The Collector's Encyclopedia of Barbie Dolls*, Collector Books, 1984.

6

The Beatles,
Musicians

Who They Are

Not all the greatest heroes of the last 50 years come with moral or political gravitas; some are simply people whose creativity and style continue to influence each successive generation. And who could have imagined the worldwide impact of a rock band that was actually just one of countless bands who crossed the pond from Britain to the United States in the 1960s? Who could have anticipated the effect of their music on generations to follow? Who could have appreciated their style and sound in the context of a wider cultural revolution? Who could have predicted the longevity of their careers both together and individually? Absolutely no one could have thought they would be so influential for so long.

The Beatles were controversial in their time–both when they first appeared on the scene and later when they were seen as embracing a lifestyle of drugs and countercultural social and political views. But now they are so mainstream that Paul McCartney has even performed during the halftime show of the Super Bowl!

What Made the Men

Among the Fab Four, John Lennon is generally credited as being the one who formed the band and was most instrumental in its development as a group. It was Lennon who found Paul McCartney and, later, George Harrison. This core group, along with a variety of drummers and other musicians that came and went, haunted the small venues of Liverpool looking for work. The band had a variety of names–almost as many as there were drummers. The Quarrymen became Johnny and the Moondogs, which begot Long John and the Beatles, which begot the Silver Beatles which begot the Beat Brothers, which finally, thankfully, begot the Beatles!

Once they had settled on a name, it was time to make a name for themselves. The music business has never been easy, but a trip to Hamburg and a chance meeting with Tony Sheridan produced their first hit, *My Bonnie*, under the name of Tony Sheridan and the Beat Brothers. However, their start in Britain really began when Brian Epstein took over as their manager and began to promote the band. It was at this time, in 1962, that the final piece fell into place: a new drummer named Ringo Starr–or, as his mother knew him, Richard Starkey. Their first hit, *Love Me Do*, finally brought the Beatles to national prominence.

It took almost a year and a half before the same song became a hit in the United States, because most record producers and radio station managers were convinced that British groups would not appeal to American audiences!

That first hit was followed by a succession of hits in Britain–*Please, Please Me, From Me to You* and *She Loves You* just for starters. Some believe that the reason American teenagers did not embrace the Beatles for so long was…their haircuts! It just was not what real rockers looked like! In the beginning, not even Dick Clark's famous *American Bandstand* could crack American audiences' indifference to this new English band.

It was Brian Epstein who came to the rescue; he arranged three gigs on the then-famous *Ed Sullivan Show*–a Sunday night staple that was watched by huge audiences. The show and the song *I Want to Hold Your Hand* were just the ticket–Beatlemania was on, and there would be no end to it. The song made it to No. 1 on the U.S. charts, and the Beatles never looked back. Perhaps the best evidence of their irrefutable success came when they arrived at New York's JFK Airport to near-riotous mobs of fans. The years 1964 and 1966 took the Beatles around the world, going on tours throughout the United States, Australia and New Zealand, Japan and the Philippines.

From 1966 to 1969 the band appeared much less in public but was experimenting musically and exhibiting great creativity in both sound and lyrics. During this period, the band produced the albums *Revolver, Sgt. Pepper's Lonely Hearts Club Band, Magical Mystery Tour, The White Album*, and *Abbey Road*. But this was also a time in which not only creative differences but also personal relationships were increasingly affecting the band's work. It is generally thought that no wedge worked more effectively to split the band apart than the presence of Yoko Ono, John Lennon's girlfriend. She began to have tremendous influence on Lennon and the direction of the band–much of which was resented by the other band members. By 1969, both Lennon and McCartney had, for all practical purposes, left the band. All that was needed was to sign the papers–which McCartney began in 1970.

Above all else, many music historians feel that it was the death from a drug overdose of their long-time business manager, Brian Epstein, in 1967 that advanced the deterioration of the band–there was no one there to manage the complex business and financial matters, and tensions within the band grew. As this period progressed, the Beatles had changed, and changed dramatically. They were more and more radical, reflecting the hippie movement and the anti-establishment feelings of the young and disenfranchised. Drugs and spiritualism became an increasing part of their lives, and their personal dissatisfactions and artistic differences only made the partnership increasingly difficult to maintain.

The Legacy of the Men

The Beatles left not only a portfolio of some of the most creative and ingenious music from the midcentury but also a series of films–many of which were critical and financial successes. There seemed nothing that they could not do. And, yet, sometimes with success, there comes a degree of arrogance and a detachment from the people and events that propel a person to success.

Of course, all of this is clear in retrospect. On one trip to the Philippines, they snubbed the powers that be–and then had cause to regret it. The band found itself barely able to get to the airport safely. Every effort was made to threaten and harass them before leaving the country. And not long after that, John Lennon proclaimed in *The Evening Standard* that the Beatles were "more popular than Jesus." Interestingly the quote caused little reaction in England but caused a furor elsewhere, especially in conservative parts of the United States. Additional comments about Christianity (that it was dying), as well as a general disregard for generally accepted beliefs and behavior (including drugs), helped further estrange the group increasingly from its fan base.

Does this suggest that all Beatles fans were now, suddenly, former fans? Not at all. In fact, part of the legacy of these heroes is that year after year their music is rediscovered by each new generation–even by those exposed to the hardest of hard rock and the most rhythm-fueled rap. The body of work itself–as well as the terrible death of John Lennon–cemented the Beatles in the minds of the music-loving public as the best and greatest ... at least until the next best and greatest comes around!

So how do we think of our heroes after some 45 years? We think of them fondly, although at times with some confusion. However, we know for a fact that they remade music as we know it. What we do not know is why they could not have continued, why were the many strange sideshow activities necessary and how such mistrust could creep in. Was it because of all the money? Were the differences a matter of artistic temperament? We may never know for sure, but we will always have the music (and the movies) to comfort us.

The Resources

Said to be the official Beatles' Website, visit *www.beatles.com* for a variety of images, words, album covers and other memorabilia from the Beatles era. A very intriguing and rich Website is called I Am The Beatles, which can be found by visiting *www.iamthebeatles.com*. For true fans, visit *www.rarebeatles.com* for interesting and obscure materials from the Beatles era.

Paul David (Bono) Hewson, *Musician*

Who He Is

How is it that an Irish rocker can influence presidents and popes, the rich, the powerful and the ordinary in such a profound way? Why is this man so very different from his contemporaries in music and entertainment? What has motivated this man to take a stand on one of the worst crises to hit the world in a thousand years?

It is not often that a very successful artist and musician takes the time and effort to work zealously for a cause, and it is particularly fascinating that the cause is Africa in general and, in particular, efforts to assist AIDS patients. The image of most rockers and superstars is that they are selfish, preoccupied with their lives, their careers, their marriages (assuming that they last more than 2 months) and their children. Superstars reek of hedonism and materialism. So what makes this man, Bono, so different? Why is he almost obsessed with the problems in Africa, and why has he given huge sums, his talent and time for this cause?

If nothing else, we need more people like him; but at the very least, we should know more about him and what makes him respond with such righteous indignation to the misery and suffering in Africa.

What Made the Man

Of course, Bono is not really Bono, nor is he Bono Vox (his full nickname), but rather Paul David Hewson, born in Dublin into a mixed family (in this case, not racial, but religious—one parent was Catholic and the other Protestant). The young man was greatly influenced (as was some of his early music) by the premature death of his mother when he was 14 years old. It was in high school that the basis of his band, U2, was formed—but not until after the name went through a number of iterations, including Feedback and Hype.

The boys—Bono, The Edge (David Evans), Adam Clayton and Larry Mullen—became an overnight success when they signed with Island Records in 1980 and released their first two albums, *Boy* and *October*. Their first change of direction, one that is decidedly more political, came when *War*, with its overtones of the Irish political troubles, was released.

Nothing about Bono makes any sense without trying to understand U2 and its music, which is so popular that since its inception in 1976, the band has sold some 50 million albums–probably a great deal more if all markets and versions are included in the figures.

> Bono was not a supporter of Irish nationalism, especially the extreme Provisional IRA; rather, the music was a call to get rid of sectarian violence and unite as the nation of the Irish, whether Catholic or Protestant.

Increasingly, U2 and Bono began to participate in more and more aid concerts, beginning with Band Aid in 1984 and Live Aid for Ethiopia in 1985. This show was seen by billions of people live through satellite feeds and was a major instigator of Bono's awareness of the needs of the people of Africa.

U2 has continued to participate in great public works of charity through a series of live concerts, as well as maintaining a superb musical career that is both creative and well respected. They are only one of four bands ever featured on Time magazine, and Rolling Stone has continued to declare U2 to be one of the greatest bands in the history of rock and roll.

But it is not specifically for his music that Bono is one of the great modern heroes. Rather, it is for his humanitarian aid and his attempts to awaken the world's consciousness about poverty and sickness in Africa specifically. His popularity as a musician and his total commitment to aid to Africa brought about a meeting with President Bush and a tour of Africa with then Treasury Secretary Paul O'Neill– though he was not in a position to influence policy.

In the same year, Bono established an organization called DATA, which stands for Debt, AIDS, Trade (in) Africa. The group's purpose was to call attention to the huge need to reduce African debt, to do something about the AIDS epidemic and improve trade in Africa. By 2005, his influence was spreading, and included efforts to increase Canadian aid to Africa, as well as a series of concerts called Live 8, the goal of which was to increase awareness and raise money for African aid. For his efforts, he was nominated as Time's Man of the Year and nominated several times for the Nobel Peace Prize.

The Legacy of the Man

How do we understand this man, Bono? What makes him tick? At a time when so many celebrities spend their time and money on themselves and on small, insignificant projects that have little meaning beyond their personal interest, what makes a man like Bono respond so differently? Bono is first of all a Christian and takes that part of Christianity that says that you must take care of the children, the poor and the widowed very seriously. (He notes that Judaism and Islam also have the same charity-based tenets and that the three religions ought to make common cause for the sake of Africa.)

A good part of his future legacy will be the fact that he has put such pressure on the economic powers to increase aid to Africa. He has clearly understood that the future is Africa–half the population is under 20 years of age. At the same time, it has some of the highest poverty in the world, especially in sub-Saharan Africa. As much as 70 percent of the population lives on less than two dollars a day, and some 200 million go hungry daily.

If one issue in Africa could be identified as the main catalyst for action, it would certainly be the AIDS epidemic. Nearly 17 million Africans have died of the disease and another 25 million are infected with it, including some 1.9 million children. Raising global consciousness about AIDS has made Bono such a powerful activist for Africa. That said, he also underlines the importance of long-term economic thinking. Immediate help is vital, but these countries also need to develop economies that can support large populations.

Along with others, Bono has pressured the great world economies to reduce African debt to the World Bank and the International Monetary Fund. Debt reduction will allow hundreds of billions of dollars to remain in Africa for development. Further, he recognizes how important trade and economic development will be to the future of Africa. Countries cannot solve AIDS or poverty unless they have the ability to develop sophisticated and sustainable economies. There is plenty of wealth in Africa; it is using this wealth for the benefit of Africans that is so important to Bono.

There are some activists who insist that Bono is too close to the leaders of government. They say that he would be more effective if he stood apart, was more critical, and if he insisted that policies be changed faster and that more money become available for aid. And of course some wags say that his social views do not hurt record and concert sales, making Bono a very rich man. If there are flaws in the man and in his views, they are seemingly not taken seriously by most people, who recognize him for his talents as a musician and his role as an activist for Africa.

The Resources

Bono's organization, DATA, has an extensive Website filled with information about its programs and its policies. Visit *www.data.org* for more information.

A new book, simply called *Bono*, Riverhead Trade, 2006, is gaining great approval among Bono fans. You can find the book at most larger bookstores, or visit *www. amazon.com* for more information.

8

Warren Buffett,
Businessman

Who He Is

To be among the top two or three richest people in the world invites heroic status. The amazing thing about Warren Buffett, however, is that he got rich not by being a robber baron or by founding some spectacular high-tech company to much public acclaim. Rather, he was an investor of quiet demeanor and habit (never did build that mega-mansion in Omaha) who viewed investing and business in the long term. Slowly and deliberately, he acquired company after company, which he folded into his holding organization, Berkshire Hathaway–the most expensive stock on the New York Stock Exchange.

What makes Warren Buffett a true hero is that he has given most of his money to charity. With one swipe of the pen, tens of billions of dollars went to a variety of good causes, mostly under the auspices of the Bill and Melinda Gates Foundation to be used in ways that will benefit the world.

He is our hero because he remains humble and retains a sense of humor, despite billions in wealth and enormous personal power and prestige. All would agree that this is a rare combination, considering the typical vast egos of the world's rich and famous!

What Made the Man

Buffett was born into an upper-middle-class family on August 30, 1930, in Omaha, Nebraska. His father, Howard, was a stockbroker and later would be a U.S. Congressman. Buffett had two sisters. His grandfather owned a grocery store in Omaha where both Warren and his friend Charlie Munger worked as boys. Munger would go on to be the president of Buffett's investment company, Berkshire Hathaway.

At an early age, Buffett was able to calculate columns of numbers in his head, a feat he still performs today. When he was 6 years old, he bought six-packs of Coca-

Cola from his grandfather's store for 25 cents, then turned around and sold the bottles for a nickel each, giving him a profit of five cents.

Although Buffett was making good money delivering newspapers in high school and had no desire to go to college, his father urged him to attend the Wharton School at the University of Pennsylvania. After two years, Buffett was complaining that he knew more about business than his professors. His father was defeated for re-election and Buffett returned home, where he graduated from College of Business Administration at the University of Nebraska.

It was there that Buffett would meet the man who would have a major influence on his future career and success as an investor. By the 1940s, Ben Graham was considered one of the most influential investors in America. He had built his reputation on careful consideration of the market and purchasing stocks at such a low price that they presented a minimal risk. He wrote the groundbreaking book *Security Analysis.* Later, he would publish *The Intelligent Investor*, which made a huge impression on Buffett.

Graham was one of Buffett's instructors at the Columbia Business College, and the young Buffett earned the only A+ Graham had ever given a student in his security analysis class. After graduation, Buffett applied for a position in the Graham & Newman investment brokerage. He was initially turned down and worked at his father's brokerage as a salesman. Graham finally hired him in 1954.

Buffett had been dating Susie Thompson in the early 1950s, and they married in 1952. They soon had a daughter, also named Susie. When Graham asked Buffett to work for him, the couple moved to suburban New York. Buffett worked tirelessly, analyzing Standard & Poor's (S&P) reports on possible investments. It was during this time that his and Graham's philosophies on investing began to diverge. Graham made his decisions solely on the basis of numbers. Buffett was more interested in how a company worked, what its business philosophy and management style were, and how it differed from the competition.

During this time, Buffett built up his own sizable funds for future investments. Graham retired from the business in 1956, and Buffett returned to Omaha to set up his own investment company. He established Buffett Associates, Ltd., and later Buffett Partnership Limited. Buffett ran all the partnerships out of his bedroom.

Buffett proved his ability by showing profits almost 50 times higher than the Dow. He soon found himself a millionaire and a father of three. Also at this time, he made an important professional decision when he hired Charlie Munger. The two shared a similar business philosophy, and Munger was instrumental in expanding Buffett Partnership.

Buffett had purchased enough stock in an undervalued manufacturing company called Berkshire Hathaway that he was made a director. In 1967, he bought the whole company and made it into the largest holding company in the world.

Buffett's business philosophy was to take profits from the company and use it to acquire other businesses or buy stock in public companies.

Although Buffett's business life was thriving, his personal life was in disarray. His wife left him, but remained married to him, and set up her own apartment in San Francisco. Buffett was devastated, but he and Susie remained close, even taking annual vacations together. Eventually Susie would introduce Buffett to a waitress named Astrid Menks. She later moved in with Buffett, all with Susie's blessings.

By the 1970s, Buffett was considered one of the most talented investors in the country. During the me decade of the 1980s, he started devoting more time to charitable efforts. He devised an innovative plan where each shareholder in his company would designate $2 for charitable giving from each Berkshire share. Eventually, Berkshire Hathaway was giving away millions of dollars each year, all to the shareholders' favorite causes.

The Buffett reputation for philanthropic giving reached new heights in 2006, when he announced that he would contribute 10 million Berkshire Hathaway Class B stocks to the Bill and Melinda Gates Foundation. At the time of the announcement, the stocks were worth almost $31 billion, making it the largest charitable contribution in history. At the same time, he also earmarked stock valued at almost $7 billion to the Susan Thompson Buffett Foundation (his wife had died in 2004) and foundations established by his children.

As he continues to operate the amazingly successful Berkshire Hathaway and pursue his charitable efforts, Buffett has made it clear that his children would not inherit any large amount of his estate. When asked about this, he answered in a way that summed up his business style: "I want to give my kids enough so they could feel that they could do anything, but not so much that they could do nothing."

The Legacy of the Man

Buffett's two most important legacies are his investment style and the management style he brings to companies he has acquired. As an investor he looks for companies that are in industries with good economic models. They should have upward earning trends with good and consistent margins, low debt-to-equity ratios, a high and consistent return on expenditures, a low maintenance cost of operations and retained earnings for growth, with prices that can be adjusted for inflation.

His management style keeps him from interfering in the running of the individual companies. Further, he is not involved in hiring and compensating top executives, and insists on careful capital management of the companies that make up his empire.

Buffett's public perception is of a successful man who mixes business with humor and is concerned with politics and the world around him. He can be a bit of a contradiction, supporting the Democratic Party, but also working as a financial adviser to the Republican Arnold Schwarzenegger during his successful run for California governor. His support of pro-choice groups has not sat well with anti-abortion supporters. He is also a noted technophobe who does not even have an e-mail address. This lack of technical sophistication has not hurt his career, and in his middle 70s, Buffett is still considered one of the most successful investors in history.

The Resources

You can find out more about Warren Buffett and the holding company he created by visiting *www.berkshirehathaway.com.*

Books by and about Buffett include *The Essays of Warren Buffett: Lessons for Corporate America*, The Cunningham Group, 2001; *The Warren Buffett Way,* Riley, 2004; *Buffett: The Making of an American Capitalist*, Main Street Books, 1996; and *Warren Buffett Speaks: Wit and Wisdom from the World's Greatest Investor,* Wiley, 1997.

9

Cesar Chavez,
Labor Organizer

Who He Is

Although Cesar Estrada Chavez is most famously associated with the plight of immigrant farmworkers, he was actually born a citizen of the United States in Yuma, Arizona. Chavez was politicized early in life. The family had to work in the fields, and Chavez learned firsthand not only of the hardships and mistreatment migrant workers received from wealthy farmers but also of an educational system that, he felt, was heavily prejudiced against Spanish-speaking students.

Chavez left school before he could attend high school, but remained devoted to learning. His office walls were filled with volumes of books covering a wide range of topics from economics and philosophy to biographies of people like Gandhi and John F. Kennedy.

In the early 1960s, based on his perceptions of the hardships borne by migrant workers, Chavez, along with fellow activist Dolores Huerta, founded the National Farm Workers Association, which eventually became the United Farm Workers (UFW). Chavez and the UFW used various means to alert Americans to the plight of the migrant farmworker. However, their most famous achievement was a series of boycotts of farm products produced by nonunion workers. These boycotts brought the UFW and Chavez national attention.

Chavez died, under what some consider mysterious circumstances, in 1993, in his birthplace of Yuma. There never has been satisfactory resolution as to how he died. Many remain very suspicious to this day.

What Made the Man

Chavez was born on March 31, 1927, near Yuma, Arizona. His father owned a small farm but was later swindled out of the land by unscrupulous white landowners. This, undoubtedly, gave Chavez his first taste of discrimination and exploitation.

His family had little choice but to become migrant farmworkers. They eventually moved to California in 1938 and settled near San Jose. He worked alongside his family in the fields. However, this, for Chavez, was not a means to eke out a living, but, rather a way out of an endless loop of poverty; he believed that if he worked hard and saved, he could eventually send his children to college and a better life.

Ironically, for a man who put a very high value on education, Chavez did not like formal schooling. He blamed this on the fact that, as a child, he spoke only Spanish and most of his teachers were Anglo. In fact, in those days it was forbidden for Latino students to speak Spanish in class and violating this rule resulted in harsh punishment.

Before he finished formal school, he had attended 37 separate schools. Some segregated the Spanish-speakers from the rest of the students. Others were integrated, though Chavez felt like he was in a cage in these schools. He dropped out of school after the eighth grade, partly due to the death of his father. To avoid having his mother work the fields, Chavez did it himself to provide an income for the family.

His exposure to discrimination did not ease when he entered the Navy in 1944, where he served for 2 years. After the war was over, and Chavez had been honorably discharged, he married Helen Fabela and settled in Delano, California. A few years after his marriage, Chavez returned to San Jose where he encountered, perhaps, the most influential person in his life: Father Donald McDonnell. Soon after, he met Fred Ross and Pete Fielding, who ran the new organization, Community Service Organization. Chavez agreed to work with Ross and Fielding and started organizing voter registration among Latinos.

After his exposure to activist politics with McDonnell and Ross, Chavez turned his skills into organizing migrant farmworkers. He knew their concerns intimately and was totally committed to getting them fair wages and helping them to pave a road to the American dream. He formed the National Farm Workers Association in 1962. By the 1970s, the organization had merged with other activist groups to become the United Farm Workers of America.

Chavez used several very effective tactics to help raise awareness of the injustices suffered by migrant farmworkers. He used symbols and education to bolster the pride of the migrant workers, telling them they were vital to the economy in general and the agriculture of California in particular. He organized strikes against specific growers. He led marches to the Texas state capital at Austin and down the Imperial and Coachella valleys to the border of Mexico.

He also organized nationwide boycotts of products grown on farms using nonunion workers, the most famous of which was the grape boycott of the late 1960s. The UFW tactics began to show success with these boycotts. By 1970, most grape growers had accepted union contracts that provided better wages and working conditions. From a small base of members at its start, the UFW had 50,000 dues-paying members by the early 1970s.

Taking a page from one of his heroes, Gandhi, Chavez used only nonviolent tactics to promote the UFW agenda. Also, like Gandhi, Chavez was willing to sacrifice himself with a series of fasts designed to prompt action by farm owners. He went on water-only fasts in 1968 and 1972. His most famous fast was in the summer of 1988 and lasted for 36 days. After he broke his fast, other activists and celebrities passed the fast along, existing on only water for several days each.

Throughout all of his efforts, Chavez and the UFW received the moral and practical support of African-American activists such as Ralph Bunche and Jesse Jackson, as well as prominent American statesmen such as Robert Kennedy, who wholeheartedly approved of what Chavez and the UFW were doing. It was thought this type of unabashed support helped immeasurably in the success of the UFW and Chavez.

The Legacy of the Man

Chavez took on his last cause shortly before his death. He had returned in April 1993 to help defend the UFW from a lawsuit by a large California producer of lettuce and vegetables. The producer wanted the UFW to pay millions in damages from a past boycott against him, and Chavez was there to plot the defense strategy and testify in court. He appeared in court on April 22, returned home afterward and then died sometime overnight of causes that were never fully identified. His official date of death is April 23, 1992.

Chavez's legacy as a man who bettered the lives of thousands of migrant workers was confirmed by the more than 50,000 mourners who honored him at the UFW field office in Delano, California, where Chavez had made his first and last public fasts. It was the largest funeral, to date, of any U.S. labor leader. Chavez was called a "special prophet of the world's farm workers" by Cardinal John Mahoney, who presided over the funeral.

Chavez was posthumously awarded the Medal of Freedom by President Bill Clinton in 1994. His birthday is celebrated as a paid holiday in California and Texas, and as a voluntary holiday in Arizona and Colorado. He is the only Mexican-American to be honored in this way. In addition, parks in the California cities of Sacramento, San Diego, Berkeley and San Jose have been renamed for him.

Undoubtedly, the death of Chavez was a difficult blow to the farmworker cause, but others have stepped up over the years to shoulder the load. His eldest son, Fernando, still tours the country speaking about his father's efforts and legacy in union organizing and fighting for the rights of farmworkers. Other officials in the UFW remain dedicated to his principles of nonviolent activism to support their causes.

Cesar Chavez, who never earned more than $5,000 a year for his efforts, and continually put his life in danger to support the causes he believed in, was called one of the most heroic figures of our time by Robert F. Kennedy.

The Resources

There are a variety of online resources on Cesar Chavez and the UFW. Many can be accessed by visiting *www.ufw.org.*

To read more about Chavez, look at one of the books he co-wrote, *Cesar Chavez: Autobiography of La Causa*, Norton, 1975. You can also read *The Moral Vision of Cesar Chavez*, Orbis Books, 2003; *Conquering Goliath: Cesar Chavez at the Beginning*, United Farm Workers, 1989; *Cesar Chavez: A Hero for Everyone*, Aladdin, 2003; and *The Fight in the Fields: Cesar Chavez and the Farmworkers Movement*, Harvest/HBJ Book, 1998.

10

Winston Churchill,
Prime Minister

Who He Is

Some would say that with an American mother and a British father, Churchill was the perfect wartime leader. He became one of the most enduring symbols of the Second World War, an image so linked with the survival of Britain and the rigors of wartime London, that he is forever remembered as one of the great heroes in one of the great struggles of all time.

He was highly educated, arrogant, complex and not always successful or appreciated–he was voted out of office even before World War II ended, despite his Herculean efforts on behalf of the people and the country. He was a man of a different era: He was part of, and believed in, the British aristocracy and the British Empire (especially the Raj in India), yet was absolutely committed to the efforts against fascism and world conquest. It was as if two different personalities existed in one man.

What Made the Man

Trying to discover the roots of Churchill's heroism in his childhood can be challenging. He was born into privilege as a child of English nobility. In the tradition of the British aristocracy, he spent most of his childhood in boarding schools. He was distant from his parents–although fascinated by his father's political career. He is said to have been a lonely, rather disappointing boy who did not do well in school (although he would one day receive the Nobel Prize in literature).

As a young man, he had decided on a military career. Like many from his class, he went to Sandhurst, the Royal Military Academy, famous for training the officers and gentlemen of the British colonial army. His first tour of duty was to India, where more time was spent in leisure than in military activity. Eager for action, he managed to find his way to Cuba and then to the Sudan, which region the British army was attempting to retake.

Interestingly, the young officer Churchill often acted as a war correspondent for various London papers. In fact, his first act of heroism occurred while working as a correspondent during the Boer War of 1899. Although eventually captured and put in a prison camp, he managed to take charge during a difficult trainwreck that threatened the lives of soldiers and passengers. He escaped from prison and made his way out of South Africa; when he returned, it was as a commissioned officer. His exploits in the Boer War made him a celebrity in Britain. Throughout this period of his life, he seems to have generated a bit of controversy. Historians are never quite sure of some of the facts or events as recounted by Churchill. He clearly was a young man who thought nothing of altering facts to fit the circumstances–or so some of his critics charged.

The year 1900 saw the beginning of his political career, when he was elected to Parliament as a Conservative. Throughout his early years, he would cause a great deal of dissatisfaction with his fellow Conservatives, to the extent that he changed sides and became a Liberal member. Although he would eventually rejoin the Conservatives, he seemed able to have it both ways–working in various Cabinet-level positions, including First Lord of the Admiralty. It was while he was First Lord that an infamous battle was planned in Turkey at Gallipoli, which turned out to be a disaster for British and Australian forces–a fiasco so serious that Churchill was forever associated with it.

It was his nature to meddle in matters in which he probably had no business being involved. As First Lord of the Admiralty, Churchill took the leadership in developing a then-unique weapon of war–the battle tank. Historians and others have questioned how the navy was expected to bear the costs for the development of the tank. Many inside and outside the government thought that this was massive misuse of departmental funds; but that, of course, did not stop Churchill.

With World War I came a new political and social experiment, the Russian form of communism (then often called Bolshevism), which made many Western leaders very nervous. Churchill was particularly alarmed by this movement and urged the government to intervene on behalf of the White Russians against the Communists. It was the nature of Churchill and his worldview that Britain should be involved in every major (and sometimes minor) regional dispute. A parallel example can be seen in his support of the Empire, particularly the jewel in the crown, India, where he fiercely opposed home rule and, of course, ultimate independence.

The whole world by this point had recognized Gandhi as a
great and good man. Churchill would have nothing to do
with him; this attitude simply reinforces the view of a man
who was stalled in a mid-19th century time warp.

If India could not have home rule, Ireland could and would. Churchill worked
with members of the government to help create the Irish Free State in the 1920s.
But his worldview became even more complicated with the advent of Mussolini
and Italian-style fascism. He admired the man and his policies, primarily as a
counter to communism. Fortunately, he did not take the same view of Hitler
and was an early and strident alarmist over German rearmament and Hitler's
worldview–a view that nevertheless held the British and their world empire in
great admiration!

Almost alone in government, he opposed appeasement with Germany and
Hitler. He was vocal in his denunciation of Neville Chamberlain and the Munich
Agreement, which gave a good part of then Czechoslovakia to Germany on the
pretext that a German minority was being abused by the Czech majority. Naturally,
history and world events would prove that appeasement would not work. The
Chamberlain government fell, and Churchill and a wartime coalition government
took over.

Stalin referred to Churchill as an English bulldog for his stubbornness and his
unwillingness to compromise. Hitler found Churchill even more difficult. With
the fall of France, Britain stood alone in 1940 as the only viable opponent of the
German war machine. It was in this context of defiance and uncompromising
belief in the invincibility of Britain that he rallied the people with his famous
blood, sweat and tears speech–one of many for which he would be famous.

If Churchill ever displayed genius, it was in his systematic courting of Franklin
Roosevelt. Britain needed U.S. aid, U.S. armaments and, most importantly, needed
the United States as an active ally in the war against Germany, Italy and Japan.
Churchill and Roosevelt began what would be called the special relationship
between the two countries. He was also the author of the Europe-first strategy
as well as an early supporter of the Atlantic Charter (the beginnings of the North
Atlantic Treaty Organization–NATO).

Postwar, Churchill found himself out of office until his political return in 1951.
He continued his fierce resistance against Stalin and communism, yet was more
than willing to protect British colonial interests in Africa, the Middle East and
Southeast Asia.

One of his most famous pronouncements was that an iron curtain was descending on Eastern Europe as the Communists took almost complete control of a third of the continent.

The Legacy of the Man

Churchill was a rogue, scholar, the ultimate politician, historian and a conservative. He saw no reason to change the world order or the British control of nearly half of it. At the same time, he exuded an almost greater-than-life connection with the British people—as though he truly was one of them in their hardship and suffering. Ironically, born to a wealthy family, he ended up with little money and used his writings and books to maintain a lavish lifestyle.

How could a man so seemingly out of touch with the contemporary world attract such enthusiasm and public acclaim? Was he perhaps the master of public image? Or is it perhaps that his words speak of a genius in public relations, history and international politics? If nothing else, his abiding legacy is that of a man willing to fill a huge void at a moment in history when the world was in chaos and on the brink of anarchy.

The Resources

The enduring hero worship of Winston Churchill by Americans is immortalized in the Washington, D.C.based organization called The Churchill Centre, which is designed for a broad base of readers and interested parties. Visit *www.winstonchurchill.org* for more details and a wonderful resource.

A thoroughly enjoyable site gives ample evidence of Churchill's cleverness and creativity. Readers can find dozens of quotes from Churchill by visiting *www.brainyquote.com.*

11

Jacques-Yves Cousteau, *Marine Biologist*

Who He Is

Anyone who has watched public television during the 1960s and 1970s knew Jacques Cousteau as that very entertaining and very special hero who brought undersea exploration into our living rooms. An environmentalist without peer, he showed us a world that we previously could just imagine. His heroic ventures are similar to space exploration: a combination of technology and sheer bravery bringing the suboceanic world to everyman.

He is even more our hero because he inspired generations to study and care for the sea, and to work to protect it for future generations. Some of his finest work revolved around the technology of sea exploration, but his most important effort, the reason he is our hero, is that he was a genuine environmentalist with all the world at heart.

What Made the Man

Jacques-Yves Cousteau was truly a man of the sea. His scientific breakthroughs in diving technology and his tireless fight against the pollution of the oceans made him a hero to a generation of future explorers and environmental activists. His voyages on his ship Calypso became the subject of books, television specials and even a hit song by John Denver.

Cousteau was born on June 11, 1910, in Saint-Andre-de-Cubzac, France, to Daniel and Elizabeth Cousteau. He began his lifelong love for the sea in 1930 when he was admitted to France's Ecole Navale (Naval Academy). He became a gunnery officer in the navy and began conducting diving experiments. His first innovation in underwater technology was the development of a better type of underwater goggles in 1936, thought to be the precursors of modern diving masks.

A year later, Cousteau married Simone Melchior and would have two sons with her: Jean-Michel and Phillippe. Both would go on to work with their father on his underwater expeditions.

Cousteau fought in World War II, but also found time to experiment with devices allowing divers to breathe underwater. Two almost-fatal accidents with rebreathers had convinced him there had to be a better and safer way to free humans from the air lines that divers traditionally used. Along with Emile Gagnan, he developed the first commercially successful diving system in 1943. Called SCUBA (self-contained underwater breathing apparatus) or the Aqua-Lung, the device used compressed air in tanks strapped to the diver's back and a regulator to breathe through. The device would revolutionize underwater work.

Cousteau began using his Aqua-Lung while still serving with the French navy in World War II. He discovered a way to use the devices for clearing mines and also began exploring underwater wrecks. Looking for new ways to show what his invention could do, Cousteau and fellow diver Frederic Dumas explored one of the deepest known underground rivers in the world. Because of a mistake in filling their tanks, the two divers almost died due to carbon monoxide poisoning. In 1967, Cousteau returned to the river where he almost met his death and sought its origin using a remote-controlled minisub called the Telenaute.

Cousteau's achievements came to the attention of Loel Guinness, president of the French Oceanographic Campaigns. Guinness had bought a decommissioned minesweeper, the Calypso, and leased the ship to Cousteau for one franc a year. During the next four decades, Calypso and Cousteau became synonymous with cutting-edge exploration of the seas. Cousteau encouraged a collegial atmosphere on the ship, with no hierarchy of officers and crew (although Cousteau was addressed by the honorific Captain).

Cousteau's early films of his explorations won three Academy Awards (for *The Silent World*, *The Golden Fish* and *World Without Sun*). In 1968, Cousteau created *The Undersea World of Jacque Cousteau*, which became one of the most popular television documentary series in history.

At the same time, Cousteau had not given up on his efforts to improve the technology for underwater exploration. He pioneered new techniques in underwater photography in the 1950s, and in 1963, along with Jean de Wouters, developed the revolutionary underwater camera, the Calypso-Phot, later licensed to Nikon, who called it the Calypso-Nikkor and then the Nikonos. Soon after, Cousteau made diving history again by creating, with Jean Mollard, the SP-350, a two-man submersible that could dive to 350 meters below the surface (the design would be upgraded in 1965 to subs that could reach 500 meters in depth).

At the same time, Cousteau's experiences exploring the oceans were making him more and more sensitive to the impact of human beings on the seas. He believed the sea was a source of material, as well as an inspiration and a source of well-being. Although he stated he never said, "The sea is dying," he was still an outspoken advocate of reducing human pollution of the seas.

His first visible campaign was to publicly oppose the planned dump of radioactive waste from EURATOM into the sea. The popular support he received resulted in public protests that included women and children blocking the tracks of the railroad that was to deliver the waste to a seaport. The train was turned back to its starting point. Cousteau would remain opposed to nuclear experiments and even had an informal debate with French president Charles de Gaulle on the subject.

With his two sons, Jean-Michel and Phillippe, Cousteau established The Cousteau Society in 1973. The society devotes itself to funding explorations by the Calypso and her sister ship the Alcyone, and promoting environmentally friendly policies for use of the seas. The society now boasts over 300,000 members.

Cousteau's first wife, Simone, died of cancer in 1990. In 1991, he married Francine Triplet (they had already had a daughter and son before the marriage– Cousteau's first family was unaware of their existence). Cousteau spent a large amount of his later years battling his son Jean-Michel for control of the Cousteau name. Tragically, his beloved Calypso sank in Singapore harbor. At the age of 87, Cousteau developed a severe respiratory illness. While recovering from it, he died of a heart attack in 1997. He was buried in the Cousteau family plot at Saint-Andre-de-Cubzac Cemetery in France and not, as is popularly believed, at sea.

The Legacy of the Man

Jacques Cousteau will always be credited with helping open the seas to human exploration. Prior to his development of the Aqua-Lung, divers were forced to free-dive without support equipment, using hard suits and connected to an air hose on the surface or relying on unpredictable and frequently unsafe rebreathers.

Cousteau excited a whole generation about the beauty, dangers and fragility of the seas. Using his Aqua-Lung, millions of people have been able to visit Cousteau's sometimes-dangerous undersea world as tourists, explorers or workers.

Cousteau referred to himself as an oceanographic technician, meaning he was first and foremost an inventor and engineer. However, his contemporaries regarded him as a man in love with nature in general and the sea in particular. He called the oceans the blue continent.

Many formally trained scientists dismissed Cousteau's explorations and so-called discoveries as publicity stunts geared more toward a popular audience than to the advancement of scientific theory. The scientific community at first also dismissed his technique of communication called divulgationisme, a simple method of sharing scientific concepts. In time, this method would be used in other disciplines and become an important part of modern television.

Cousteau's work was honored on several occasions. He received the United Nations Environmental Prize in 1977 (along with Peter Scott), was awarded the Presidential Medal of Freedom in 1985 from Ronald Reagan and was a regular consultant for the United Nations and World Bank.

After Cousteau's death, Jean-Michel and his son, Fabien, carried on underwater explorations and created documentaries about the sea. They released a new series, *Ocean Adventures in 2006*, one episode of which, *Voyage to Kure*, inspired President George W. Bush to establish the Northwestern Hawaiian Islands National Monument, the largest marine protected zone in the world.

The Resources

Almost all of the documentaries created by Jacques Cousteau and his son are available on DVD and videocassette. The No. 1 song *Calypso* by John Denver is available on the CD of the same name. You can find more information on The Cousteau Society at *www.cousteau.org*.

There are many books written by and about Cousteau, including *Jacques Cousteau: The Ocean World*, Harry N. Abrams, 1985; *Jacques Cousteau: A Biography*, Lerner Publishing Group, 2000; *Silent World*, National Geographic, 2004; *The Ocean World of Jacques Cousteau (20 Volumes)*, Danbury Press, 1975; and *Jacques Cousteau and the Undersea World*, Chelsea House Publications, 2000.

12

Walter Cronkite, *Anchorman*

Who He Is

There was a time, not so long ago, when network news broadcasts in the evening were the most powerful on television. The men (and they were all men) who presented the news were icons to the American public. Walter Cronkite was the dean of television newsmen, reciting the day's events with grace and poise, and with a solemnity that they deserved. There was no cable, no instant messaging, no Internet, no streaming news. There was only Walter and men like him.

At the height of his career, he was the most admired and trusted man in the United States. If Walter Cronkite said it, it must be true. He is our hero because he never gave us cause to mistrust him; he never abused the faith we put in him, or became haughty or proud. He always remained the same: the good and righteous man who would interpret a complex world for us every evening.

What Made the Man

Although he was a legitimate star, Cronkite insisted he was an ordinary working journalist and used the values he learned growing up in the Midwest to temper his reporting on some of the most compelling and controversial issues of the 20th century.

He was born on November 4, 1916, in St. Joseph, Missouri. The family later moved to Houston, Texas, in 1928. After graduating high school, he attended the University of Texas at Austin, but dropped out in his junior year. He spent a brief time in 1935 covering news and sports for a local Austin newspaper and working in public relations. He moved into broadcast journalism in 1936 as an announcer for WKY in Oklahoma City, Oklahoma.

He fell in love with his future wife, Mary Elizabeth Maxwell, while he was a sports announcer for KCMO-AM in Kansas City, Missouri. They would marry soon after.

In the early days of radio, broadcasters were not allowed to use their real names because the station owners were afraid the announcers would take listeners with them if they moved to another station. During his first stint as a broadcaster, Cronkite's on-air name was Walter Wilcox.

Cronkite's big career break came during World War II. He joined the reporting staff of the United Press (UP). He became part of a group of war journalists known as the Writing 69th. Cronkite showed he would do almost anything to get a story, including going ashore on D-Day, making parachute landings with the 101st Airborne and accompanying bombing missions to Germany. Cronkite raised his profile even higher when he was the UP reporter covering the postwar Nuremberg Trials of suspected Nazi war criminals. After that, he opened the first postwar UP office in Moscow, where he stayed for 2 years.

CBS news legend Edward R. Murrow, who achieved fame during his coverage of the London Blitz, recognized an extraordinary newsman in Cronkite and tried to get him to join the CBS radio news team during the war. Cronkite chose to stay with UP for the time being. Finally, he accepted an offer to work for CBS in 1950. The term anchor was coined for Cronkite's work coordinating the first live national television coverage of the Democratic and Republican national conventions in 1952.

He covered other high-profile events for CBS radio and television, and hosted the television program *You Are There*. This show re-created historical moments, the twist being that the events were covered by television as they would be in the 1950s. Cronkite created a memorable last line for the show: "What sort of day was it? A day like all days, filled with those events that alter and illuminate our lives … and you were there."

CBS rewarded Cronkite for his hard work and obvious talent on camera by making him the successor to Douglas Edwards as the anchorman of the *CBS Evening News* in 1962. At the time the show was only 15 minutes long but was expanded to 30 minutes less than a year after Cronkite took over.

Thanks to a combination of financial support of the news division by CBS and Cronkite's own experience as a wartime reporter, the *CBS Evening News* soon emerged as the leader in national news shows and gave CBS a reputation for both trustworthiness and in-depth reporting.

Ironically, one of Cronkite's first on-air interviews in the new 30-minute format was with President John F. Kennedy. Barely 2 months later, Cronkite was the first on the air with news of Kennedy's shooting and death. One of the most memorable moments in television broadcast history happened as a visibly shaken Cronkite seemed to choke up on camera when announcing the death of the president. He later admitted he almost did not make it through the broadcast because he was so upset.

Another national tragedy that would define Cronkite's reputation was the Vietnam War. He was originally quite hawkish on the war but managed to maintain a balanced news approach. As the war dragged on and the American death toll kept rising, Cronkite became more disillusioned with Vietnam. He traveled to the country to cover the Tet Offensive and returned to editorialize on the air, expressing his belief that the war was unwinnable. President Johnson reportedly said after Cronkite's remarks, "If I've lost Walter Cronkite, I've lost the country."

Johnson dropped out of the presidential race, although no one can be certain it was directly related to Cronkite's dismissal of the war.

During this period, Cronkite stayed busy hosting other news-related television series, including *Twentieth Century*, *Eyewitness to History* and *21st Century*. During the tumultuous election year of 1968, Cronkite anchored the violent and chaotic Democratic convention in Chicago. When Dan Rather was physically harassed by security guards, Cronkite said on air, "I think we've got a bunch of thugs here, Dan."

Cronkite was famously associated with the NASA manned space program and especially the Apollo program, barely able to hide his enthusiasm for what was being achieved in space. During the first moon landing mission of Apollo 11 in 1969, Cronkite was on the air 27 of the 30 hours it took for Apollo 11 to complete its mission. When Neil Armstrong descended the LEM ladder to the moon, all Cronkite could get out in terms of commentary were, "Wow!" and "Oh, boy!"

Under CBS's mandatory retirement system, Cronkite left the anchor chair in 1981 and was succeeded by Dan Rather. Cronkite has stayed very active in journalism, writing syndicated columns and broadcasting as a special correspondent for CBS, CNN and National Public Radio. Cronkite survived quadruple bypass surgery in 1997 and soon returned to an active life.

The Legacy of the Man

Walter Cronkite's legacy as a consummate professional journalist and influential broadcaster will, perhaps, never be surpassed, especially in an era when news is readily available from cable television and the Internet.

Besides his continuing on-air work, he helped found the Walter Cronkite School of Journalism and Mass Communication at Arizona State University.

He has also been more politically outspoken since his official retirement. He publicly befriended President Bill Clinton during his impeachment, supported gay marriage and has repeatedly voiced his opposition to President George W. Bush's invasion of Iraq.

Cronkite was not universally admired by other broadcast journalists. Many believed he did not take enough risks, relied too much on short, breaking stories rather than in-depth pieces and spent too much time center stage during the nightly news broadcasts.

In the current environment, Cronkite, like others in the national media, has been criticized by more politically conservative observers as being biased to both Democratic and liberal causes. No hero is ever free from some controversy!

To most Americans, however, Cronkite was one of the few people who could be trusted during a disturbing period in the nation's history, and the fact is that much of the country believed him when he ended each broadcast with, "And, that's the way it is . . . ."

The Resources

Compilations of Cronkite's television series and copies of his specials are available on DVD and VHS. He has published his autobiography, *A Reporter's Life,* (Knopf, 1996).

Cronkite has also created a number of audiocassettes and CDs of his broadcasts and other significant moments in news, including *Cronkite Remembers,* Simon and Schuster, 2000; *Walter Cronkite's Greatest Shows of the 20th Century*, Radio Spirits, 2003; and *The United States Constitution: Constitutional Convention and the Ratification Debates*, Knowledge Products, 1987.

Charles de Gaulle, *President*

13

Who He Is

Charles de Gaulle may truly be said to be the founder of modern France. He led
the nation to becoming a major player in world affairs during and after World
War II. And though contemporaries and political enemies thought of him as the
imperial French general and statesman whose increasing political independence
alienated traditional allies, the French people nonetheless swooned with respect
and delight at everything he did or said.

A French national hero almost on a par with Napoleon, de Gaulle was larger
than life–a relatively obscure tank officer who became the president of the Fifth
Republic. To the observer, the years of his ascent and presidency are fascinating
and frustrating, marked by imperialism, arrogance and political gamesmanship as
he changed French thought and France's role in the world economy and political
sphere.

What Made the Man

Charles de Gaulle came from a traditionally Catholic background (born in 1890
in Lille, France). He was fascinated by everything French as a young man, so it
probably came as no surprise that he took a military education, graduating from
the Ecole Militaire in 1912. This was the prelude to an entire life spent in service
to France and its military.

Like most young men of his generation, he served in the massive French army
of World War I, during which he was wounded and captured by the Germans.
Between the wars, he stayed with his military career, advancing up the ladder and
spending a lot of time thinking and writing about military and political affairs.
France and her politicians were obsessed with national security, and with the
political and economic control of a smaller, now weaker Germany. After all,

France had fought Germany (or its various versions, such as Prussia) for generations.

At the time, the great minds in France felt that fixed fortifications—the Maginot Line—were the solution to everything. The French built these massive fortifications with stationary guns facing Germany. Of course, in the next war, the Germans simply went around the fixed fortifications and were in Paris within months.

De Gaulle, ever the iconoclast, wrote regularly explaining why the Maginot was the wrong strategy and that only a mechanized and specialized army (with a strong air force) would provide real protection to France. His theories were soundly rejected by his superiors—which is probably the reason that his military career did not advance beyond that of a colonel between the wars.

Like great men and heroes of all generations, it was world events that in many ways made the man. World War II was the stage that would propel de Gaulle from obscurity to prominence. Once the German advance through Belgium and Holland was complete, it was only a matter of time until the poorly defended French capitulated. For his part, de Gaulle would have none of it. He pleaded with his superiors in the army and with politicians to flee France and set up a government in absentia in North Africa.

He worked with Churchill in England on a scheme to combine the two countries and their armies for the duration of the war. Marshall Petain, the French hero from World War I and now head of government, arranged an armistice with Germany. The pro-German Vichy government was formed and de Gaulle fled to England to lead the charge for a continued French war effort. In the eyes of many, the creation of the Free French forces was a symbol of a free and independent France.

Even at this very early stage of development, the so-called French government in exile exhibited an often-frustrating need to be or at least appear to be independent of the Allied forces during the war. Churchill generally supported de Gaulle. Roosevelt, on the other hand, found de Gaulle outrageous, difficult and arrogant—probably much as Roosevelt would be in similar circumstances.

As the war progressed, Charles de Gaulle not only represented the Free French but was also considered the leader of French resistance on the continent. He used this status to gain a prominent position in postwar French politics. By 1944, his Committee for National Liberation was the provisional government of postwar France. Unfortunately, a formal process for the new government could not be agreed upon, and de Gaulle resigned. He watched (impatiently) as the Fourth Republic–with its exhausting problems in Algeria and Vietnam–collapsed. As the only national hero with sufficient prominence, he waited for the people to call. And they did.

As a condition for coming back as head of government, de Gaulle demanded that the constitution be revised and that he be given sufficient emergency powers to institute economic and political reforms. He became, with overwhelming popular approval, the Fifth Republic, enacting strong economic reforms, dramatically centralizing control over many domestic issues and almost completely controlling international affairs. He had the potential to be a near dictator, if he so chose. He did not.

Few people outside France can understand the historical role of the French colonies, especially the importance of Algeria, in the national psyche. The geographical and political entity called France was defined by more than just its presence in Europe; it included French colonies around the world.

Algeria, especially, was considered part of France. When Algerian nationals started a civil war, they literally almost destroyed the national fabric of France. Military revolt, terrorism and political chaos resulted. Few Frenchmen wanted to give up Algeria; even fewer wanted to make the military and financial sacrifice of a prolonged civil war. The hero of the day was de Gaulle, but only if his role is taken in historical context. At the time, his decision to allow Algerian independence was considered by many as treason. Several attempts were made on his life. But in 1962, de Gaulle arranged a cease-fire with the Algerian National Liberation Front, and Algerian independence was approved in a popular referendum in France. It was widely conceded even by critics hostile to de Gaulle that he had succeeded in ending a crisis that no other French political leader had been able to resolve. Soon, all other French colonies in Africa were also granted independence.

But the hero would not stay a hero for long. In his second term as president, he faced increasing opposition for his high-handed political maneuvering. He made every effort possible to concentrate political power in himself and his supporters. If his stature at home was weakening, the enthusiasm of his allies and his enemies was increasingly hostile. De Gaulle did everything possible to separate France from American and British economic and political control. He refused to support the UK's admittance into the European Union, and was repeatedly and often at odds with Washington over matters of foreign policy. His insistence that France develop its own nuclear program was a direct effort to assert France's position in the world.

By 1968, his political capital at home had been used up. Inflation and a bad economy sent hundreds of thousands of students, farmers and radicals onto the streets of Paris to protest government policies and the economy. Attempts at reform failed and de Gaulle resigned the presidency in 1969. By 1970 he would be dead, nearly penniless–he never did manage to accumulate wealth, despite his personal and professional successes.

The Legacy of the Man

How should we view the man and his legacy to France and the world? If for no other reason, he is a national hero because of his unfailing belief in France, its culture and its people. He absolutely refused to allow France to become a second-rate country with a failing economy and little influence beyond Europe. His political views ensured that France and Europe would maintain independence from the two political extremes–the United States and the Soviet Union.

Some contemporaries and historians viewed his maverick ways with disdain, insisting that they were merely a reflection of the arrogance of the man himself. He personally was uncompromising and so were his domestic and international policies. In the end, however, many would accept that he was the founder of modern France. He stubbornly maintained a French political identity, including the importance of the European Union and French dominance of that Union.

The Resources

A number of very readable biographies have been published about de Gaulle over the years, including *The Last Great Frenchman: A Life of General de Gaulle*, Wiley, 1997.

The French embassy in the United States has some interesting information about de Gaulle. Visit *www.info-france-usa.org*.

14

Diana,
Princess of Wales

Who She Is

Diana is our hero because she was a larger-than-life figure, both in the United States (with its history of fascination with the British monarchy) and worldwide. Even in death, which only strengthened her heroic status, this seemingly self-absorbed woman of British nobility generated endless speculation about her thoughts, actions and desires.

She garnered great pity and compassion, despite her exalted status and seemingly charmed life. Fans worldwide could never get enough of her. The pressures to be perfect and to act like a future queen were intense—and the public knew it.

What Made the Woman

It seemed that the whole world watched the wedding of Lady Diana Spencer and Charles, the Prince of Wales. It was considered one of the fairy-tale love stories of the century. The sad reality was that the marriage was almost doomed from the start and would end in charges and countercharges of adultery, rumors of scandals, divorce and, ultimately, tragic death. Yet despite her personal problems, Princess Diana still symbolized a glamor and style that helped her in her work for several charities.

Diana Frances Spencer was born on July 1, 1961, at Park House near Sandringham, England. Her parents were members of the British aristocracy and at the time of Diana's birth were the Viscount and Viscountess Althorp. With two older sisters, Jane and Sarah, Diana was the youngest daughter in the family. A younger brother, Charles, would enter the family soon.

Her parents were considered a glamorous match (with Queen Elizabeth II attending the wedding). However, the marriage would end in divorce when Diana was only six. Many consider this traumatic experience to be one of the causes of Diana's feelings of insecurity.

Diana was sent to Riddlesworth Hall boarding school after her parents' divorce. She excelled at sports, but was not very successful in her academics. After graduation from boarding school, she headed to London to work as a nanny, as a cook and finally as an assistant at the Young England Kindergarten in Knightsbridge. By this time, her father had remarried a daughter of Barbara Cartland, the world-famous writer of romances.

Meanwhile Charles, Prince of Wales and next in line for the British throne, was under increasing pressure to marry. As the 1980s approached, Charles was nearing his mid-30s. He had been advised by male relatives to marry an innocent young woman who would place him on a pedestal. Also, in order to get his family's approval, he would have to marry someone with an aristocratic background, a Protestant and, preferably, a virgin.

Rumor has it that his future mistress and second wife, Camilla Parker Bowles, helped him find the 19-year-old Diana when she was working at Young England. Speculation spread quickly that Charles was going to marry Lady Diana and, after efforts from the palace to downplay the relationship, the engagement was officially announced on February 24, 1981.

From the beginning there were doubts from family, friends and royal observers that this was a match made in heaven. Charles and Diana seemed to have little in common and there was a 13-year age gap between them. It came out after the marriage hit the rocks that Charles had confided in a friend that before the wedding he did not love Diana, but was sure he could in time.

The wedding, in full royal splendor, took place on July 29, 1981, in front of 3,500 invited guests. More than 600,000 people lined the route from Buckingham Palace to the cathedral. And the world watched the event on TV.

Diana quickly fell into the expected routine of visits to nurseries, schools and hospitals. The public, both in England and around the world, seemed to fall in love with the young and energetic princess. She had her first son, William, within a year of her wedding and her second son, Henry, 2 years after that.

It seemed a perfect life. However, underneath much was not going well for Diana. She suffered from postpartum depression after the birth of William. Her tendency to bulimia nervosa returned and she reportedly made a half-hearted attempt at suicide before William was born. Things worsened in the marriage through the rest of the 1980s and early 1990s with the royal couple spending more and more time apart. Diana suspected that Charles had maintained a romantic relationship with the married Camilla Parker Bowles. He later admitted an extramarital affair with Bowles.

The press was now publishing information regarding not only Charles' relationship, but also the several affairs Diana reportedly had while she was married. Throughout it all, Diana continued her efforts to assist AIDS charities (she was one of the first celebrities photographed hugging an AIDS victim) and also to promote the efforts to rid the world of unexploded landmines.

Under pressure from the queen, Charles and Diana were finally divorced on August 28, 1996. Diana told a friend it was the saddest day in her life. Because of the divorce, she lost the title Her Royal Highness and was identified now as Diana, Princess of Wales. She would never ascend to be queen.

The press was soon speculating on her apparent relationship with Dodi Fayed, the son of millionaire businessman Mohammed Al Fayed. The elder Fayed's assets included the London department store, Harrods. He continually resented what he considered to be snubs from the British upper class.

Reportedly, Diana and Dodi were deeply in love, and he was going to ask her to marry him. The couple took a brief holiday in Sardinia but were hounded constantly by the paparazzi, whom Diana had grown to resent deeply. They cut their holiday short and traveled to Paris, where the local paparazzi took up the chase.

On August 31, 1997, the couple left their hotel late at night to travel to Villa Windsor. They were driven by one of Fayed's men and were accompanied by bodyguard Trevor Rees-Jones. The paparazzi pursued the vehicle into the Pont de l'Alma road tunnel, where Diana's car, traveling at a great speed, crashed into a pillar in the tunnel. The driver and Dodi Fayed were killed instantly. Diana suffered massive internal bleeding and was taken to a hospital, where she died soon after. Only Rees-Jones survived.

The tragic death and funeral again captured the world's attention. Diana was laid to rest on an island in an ornamental lake on the grounds of Althorp Park, her family home.

The Legacy of the Woman

Despite her real concerns and efforts to help significant charities, Diana, Princess of Wales, will unfortunately be mostly remembered for what she was not. She was lovely, vivacious and glamorous, but she did not have the stamina to deal with the pressures of a royal marriage. She knew that her husband did not love her and found solace with other men in relationships that were destructive.

This sadness and vulnerability are doubtless part of Diana's continuing legacy, rather than any specific deeds she accomplished. It is impossible to say what her life might have been like if she had married Dodi Fayed.

As with the rest of her life, Diana's death was the cause of controversy. The elder Fayed was convinced the deaths were part of a conspiracy, although these theories were rejected by both British and French investigators. In 2006, an independent inquiry by Lord Stevens, former chief of the Metropolitan Police, reported the case was more complex than previously thought, although no details have been released.

Diana's life and death showed the world that, despite the best of intentions and well-wishings, fairy tales in real life do not always end happily ever after.

The Resources

A candid interview with Diana is available on a DVD, *NBC Presents: The Diana No One Knew*, Genius Entertainment, 2006. You can find information on Diana and other British royalty at *www.royal.gov.uk*.

Other books on Diana include *Diana: The Last Word*, St. Martin's Press, 2005; *The Murder of Princess Diana*, Kensington Publishing Corporation, 2004; *Diana: Her True Story in Her Own Words*, Pocket, 1998; and *Diana: Story of a Princess*, Atria, 2003.

15

Walt Disney, *Animator*

Who He Is

It many ways, it is not Walt Disney who is our hero, but the characters and animation that he and his early team created. Disney the creator continues to live every time Bambi or Snow White is re-released and another generation enjoys what the man created.

He is our hero because he left us with a legacy that can be enjoyed time and again, because he knew how to entertain us so well, and because he developed a process for creating animated films that survives even now. We marvel at his creativity, and we are thrilled every time we go to an amusement park that bears his name.

What Made the Man

The name Disney has become synonymous with innovative, family-oriented work in a variety of media—animation, live action films, television and theme parks.

Disney, a descendant of Irish immigrants, was born on December 5, 1901, in Chicago, Illinois. His father, Elias Disney, worked several jobs in Chicago and was one of the army of workers who constructed the World's Columbian Exposition of 1893.

The family left Chicago in 1906 for Marceline, Missouri. It was here that Disney developed his love for drawing. After his father was stricken with typhoid fever in 1909, the family moved to Kansas City, Missouri. Disney attended public school and also enrolled in weekend classes at the Kansas City Art Institute. Art school did not suit Disney; he spent more time doodling than listening to the lessons.

The family returned to Chicago and Disney attended McKinley High School as well as taking night courses at the Art Institute of Chicago. He dropped out of high school to join the Army and fight in World War I. He was rejected for the Army, but later joined the Red Cross Ambulance Corps. He never saw any combat. He was discharged from the Army in 1919 and returned to the United States.

His father would not support Disney in his dream of becoming an artist, so he struck out on his own and moved back to Kansas City. He worked on newspaper ads and tried to start his own art business, called Iwerks-Disney (Ub Iwerks was a good friend and fellow artist). The venture failed, and Disney ended up working at a company called Kansas City Film Ad–creating crude animated ads for local movie theaters. This is where Disney began expanding his horizons as an animator and experimenting with new techniques.

After a couple of years, he started another company, Laugh-O-Gram Films, Inc., producing short cartoons based on fairy tales and popular children's stories. Disney's innovation was to give the old material a modern spin. He employed animators who would go on to become great successes in Hollywood: his friend Iwerks, as well as Hugh Harman, Rudolph Ising, Carmen Maxwell and Friz Freleng. When Laugh-O-Gram went under he took a copy of *Alice in Wonderland*, a mixture of animation and live action, to California to try his luck in Hollywood.

A New York distributor saw his *Alice in Wonderland* and wanted to set up a deal for more live action/animated films. Disney recruited his brother, Roy, to help with the business side of his studio. The partnership would last until Disney's death. Another employee, Lillian Bounds, caught Disney's eye and the two were married in 1925.

Disney began working with distributor Charles B. Mintz on the popular *Oswald the Lucky Rabbit* series. After Mintz refused to raise the fees for Disney's work on Oswald, Disney had to find a new character.

No matter whether it was Disney or Iwerks who came up with the idea, it was Iwerks who directed the first films with a new character called Mortimer, later to be renamed Mickey Mouse by Disney's wife.

The Mickey Mouse silent cartoons could not find a distributor, but Disney reinvented animation by creating *Steamboat Willie*, the first sound animated cartoon (Disney did the vocal effects and provided the voice of Mickey until 1947). The cartoon was a smash hit.

In 1932, Disney created the *Silly Symphonies* series of animated all-music shorts. The first color *Silly Symphony* won the first Academy Award for Best Short Subject: Cartoons. Disney also received a special Academy Award in 1932 for his creation of Mickey Mouse. The series would soon spin off such immortal characters as Donald Duck, Goofy, Pluto and Minnie Mouse.

But, Disney had bigger ambitions. In 1934, he began plans for *Snow White and the Seven Dwarfs*, the first animated feature. The rest of Hollywood deemed it Disney's folly, but the end result was a triumph. Audiences flocked to the movie, and it was the highest-grossing film of 1938.

Unfortunately, later animated features such as *Pinocchio* and *Fantasia* were box office disappointments. Disney kept his head above water with a series of films that packaged together existing shorts, and resumed work on *Alice in Wonderland* and *Peter Pan*. The studio also started a series of nature films called *True-Life Adventures*.

On a trip to Chicago in the late 1940s, Disney began making drawings of his dream theme park as a way to pass the time. He would end up spending 5 years of his life developing the concept and finding suitable land to build on in Anaheim, California. He also insisted the park be surrounded by a railroad. Disneyland opened in 1955 and was an immediate success.

While still creating full-length and short animated classics, Disney Studios now started making more and more live-action films such as *20,000 Leagues Under the Sea*, *The Parent Trap* and *The Shaggy Dog*. The live-action films would reach their height with the 1964 production of *Mary Poppins*.

Disney then turned his attention to the rapidly growing medium of television. He created the daytime children's series *The Mickey Mouse Club*, and a weekly show called *Disneyland* evolved into *Walt Disney Presents*, *Walt Disney's Wonderful World of Color* and *The Wonderful World of Disney*.

Disney was now working on his grandest venture ever, The Florida Project. Disney had purchased large amounts of land near Orlando and envisioned a vastly expanded Magic Kingdom with adjacent hotels and resorts. The most compelling idea was to create a futuristic city from the ground up that was to be called the Experimental Prototype Community of Tomorrow (EPCOT).

Sadly, Disney would never see his dream fulfilled. He died of lung cancer in 1966. Roy Disney, who took over the Disney empire, insisted the Florida park be named Walt Disney World in honor of his late brother.

The Legacy of the Man

Walt Disney created an entertainment empire that, during its height, has not seen its equal. Disney was not a skilled artist, but he recognized talent in others. He had big dreams and was not afraid to fulfill them.

Disney was a hero with an edge. He was notoriously stubborn and hard to please and was always surrounded by a corps of yes-men who would carry out any order that their boss flung out.

Disney was also fiercely anti-labor, due, in part, to an animators' strike that crippled the production of *Dumbo*. He never forgave those he thought were traitors to him. He testified before the House Un-American Activities Committee (HUAC) in 1947 that some of his animators were communist agitators. He also spied for the FBI on union activity in Hollywood and engaged in illegal intimidation of labor organizers.

However, he also engaged in his philanthropic efforts, including one of his most enduring legacies, the California Institute of the Arts (CalArts), which is still sustained by Disney money. In such projects can be found evidence of a man interested in more than just business and animation.

While Disney was undoubtedly proud of the art of his animation, of the amazing technology of his theme parks and of his innovative use of television, he most likely would have wanted to be remembered for what he was: one of the greatest entertainment figures in American history.

The Resources

Most of Disney's animated and live-action films are available on VHS and DVD. There have been dozens of books published about his career, his art and the theme parks. You can find a variety of information on the man and his work at *www.disney.go.com*.

You can read more about Walt Disney in *Walt Disney: An American Original*, Disney Editions, 1994; *Inside the Dream: The Personal Story of Walt Disney*, Disney Editions, 2001; *Art of Walt Disney*, Harry N. Abrams, 1999; and *Walt Disney: Conversations*, University Press of Mississippi, 2006.

Doctors Without Borders,
Humanitarian Organization

Who They Are

What can be said about men and women, professionally trained, who are willing to go to the worst places in the world—many terribly unsafe—and perform miracles for the poorest and the sickest among us? If these people are not heroes, who is?

Doctors Without Borders helps people of all countries, regardless of political considerations. And their service is not merely a form of triage, an immediate reaction to immediate events; they also try to establish long-term care programs and facilities. In the modern world, there are few humanitarians so dedicated and so heroic.

What Made the Organization

Created in France, Doctors Without Borders is also known as Médecins Sans Frontières (MSF). It has achieved worldwide fame and recognition by providing free medical services to crisis spots around the world, both as the result of political oppression and from natural disasters. For this story, the group will be referred to as MSF.

MSF is not the first group to offer food and medical aid to those in need. Prior to its organization, a charitable group called Oxfam helped—and continues to help—alleviate suffering. Also, the International Committee of the Red Cross (ICRC), established during the American Civil War, was a primary source of aid.

The ICRC came under criticism for its perceived lack of response to the Nazi holocaust during World War II, and MSF co-founder Bernard Kouchner criticized the ICRC for its consistent neutrality, charging it with complicity in some situations.

The concept of the MSF began in the late 1960s during the Nigerian civil war. Rebels had created an independent region in the southeast area of Nigeria called

Biafra. The Nigerian government blockaded the region, and France became the only Western nation to support the rebels.

Along with other doctors, Kouchner volunteered with the ICRC to help in Biafran aid, but he chafed about having to sign a volunteer agreement that he considered a gag order. Although he witnessed many atrocities during his service, he could not communicate with the rest of the world as long as he was associated with the ICRC. When he returned to France, he criticized the Nigerian government and the ICRC. He called for international support of the country and concluded, along with similar-thinking doctors, that a new organization was needed that would concentrate on victims without regard to political and religious boundaries.

MSF was founded by combining two organizations: the Groupe d'Intervention Médicale et Chirurgicale en Urgence and the Secours Médical Français (founded by Raymond Borel). MSF's first aid mission was to Nicaragua in 1972 to help victims of an earthquake. Later, the organization would set up its first long-term medical relief mission after Hurricane Fifi devastated Honduras in 1974. The organization helped in hospitals during the Lebanese civil war in the 19 assisted victims of the Khmer Rouge in Cambodia.

The group split on what they called witnessing (the need to talk publicly about problems and events they encountered) after the election of Claude Malhuret as the MSF president in 1977. Supporters of Kouchner believed MSF should speak out about what volunteers experienced during their relief efforts, while Malhuret's supporters advocated that criticism of a government should be avoided. This debate is still going on within the organization.

MSF expanded its operations in the 1980s by engaging in aggressive fundraising efforts and setting up operational sections throughout Europe, Japan and Australia. These efforts at expansion were maintained through the 1990s and into the 21st century.

The organization also streamlined its methods of operations. An MSF team now visits a possible relief site before a field mission is established. They evaluate the level of safety and what type of aid is needed. A field mission is then set up, comprising a mission head, section coordinators (including logistics, security and vehicle maintenance), and actual surgeons and doctors to work directly with victims.

In the most visible area of medical assistance, MSF doctors and hygienists provide immediate care for the wounded, establish programs of vaccinations, treat victims of HIV/AIDS, work with local hospitals to improve sanitation (especially with providing clean water) and help with establishing long-term medical care programs to those traditionally ignored. MSF also addresses the important areas of malnutrition brought on by war conditions. It does this through the establishment of Therapeutic Feeding Centres that monitor the nutrition of children and adults and provide direct help.

Besides actual treatment, MSF keeps careful statistics on humanitarian emergencies, so that information can be better communicated to the rest of the world. The activities of MSF may be greatly appreciated by the victims they serve, but they are often viewed harshly by the governments that the organization criticizes. Besides the dangers to volunteers from stray bullets, land mines or disease, MSF volunteers are sometimes killed or kidnapped for political motives.

Occasionally, a government will expel an entire MSF field mission for exposing its atrocities to the world.

The Legacy of the Organization

MSF has received praise throughout the world for its humanitarian activities and won the 1999 Nobel Peace Prize. As the group grew and gained international prominence, it established a reputation in some of the most dangerous areas of the world.

MSF arrived in Srebrenica in Bosnia-Herzegovina as part of a UN convoy in1993, only 1 year after the Balkan Wars had begun. MSF was the only organization providing medical care to the civilians surrounding the war zones. It was forced to leave the area in 1995 under pressure from the Bosnian army.

In 1994, MSF was to experience one of its heaviest casualties when it joined the ICRC to help victims of the genocide in Rwanda. The combined effort made MSF move closer to the position of neutrality that had been maintained by the ICRC. Both groups suffered for their service, with the ICRC losing 56 and the MSF almost 100 of their local staff. The MSF demanded a military intervention at the time, but this did not occur. Later, the MSF would still criticize the actions of some governments (such as Chechnya in 1999), but has shied away from calling for military action.

Possibly one of the most significant missions the MSF took up during the 1990s was in Sierra Leone, which was involved in a bloody civil war. Not only did the MSF volunteers help in the immediate treatment of war victims, it also established long-term care programs for after the war.

Ongoing missions of the MSF include providing humanitarian support in Kosovo and Chechnya; long-term care services in Colombia as the government battles the rebels FARC; efforts in Haiti to help in surgery and in rebuilding water and waste management systems; and its activities in the Kashmir conflict in northern India (including a major element of psychological support).

Africa has been keeping MSF very busy during the last few years with relief missions to battle the spread of HIV/AIDS in sub-Saharan Africa; providing aid to the Congo during its long-running series of civil wars; working in Uganda in the war between the government and rebel guerrillas; and establishing field missions in the violent country of Côte d'Ivoire. As with other efforts, MSF combines immediate care with vaccinations, preventing the spread of disease and improving basic sanitary conditions.

One of the most recent and demanding programs established by the MSF is the campaign for Access to Essential Medicines. The campaign identifies essential medicines for a particular country's needs and tries to supply enough to fight a disease common to a certain population. Owing to the costs of prescription drugs, MSF has sometimes found itself without effective medications during its field missions and has created the campaign to encourage governments and pharmaceutical companies both to lower prices for essential medicines and to increase their supply.

Although the organization may have strayed from its founder's vision of a humanitarian group that could speak out about what its volunteers witnessed, MSF has remained one of the most independent and productive humanitarian aid groups in the world, and continues to attract a core of committed volunteers to help in their sometimes dangerous activities.

The Resources

You can find information on MSF's history, activities and funding at *www. doctorswithoutborders.com.*

Books on the organization include *Hope in Hell: Inside the World of Doctors Without Borders*, Firefly Books, 2004; *Touched by Fire: Doctors Without Borders in a Third World Crisis*, McLelland and Stewart, 1998; *Healing Our World: Inside Doctors Without Borders*, Fitzhenry and Whiteside, 2006; and *Doctors Without Borders*, PowerKids Press, 2002.

17

Dwight David (Ike) Eisenhower,
5-Star General & President

Who He Is

I like Ike was the chant of the elections in the 1950s, and there was a reason why the world liked Ike: He was a national and international hero, the supreme commander of the Allied forces and the victor over fascism in Europe. What is not to like and admire?

There was a quiet effectiveness about this man that made him a hero. Both as a general and as a politician, he always took the high road. Even though he suffered by comparison to his highly popular and energetic successor, the tag that he did little is both misleading and historically not correct. We admired him for his determination, respected him for his integrity, and most of all revered him for seeing us through one of the most turbulent times in our history.

What Made the Man

It is often said that throughout its history, the United States has been able to find the right man at the right time. This is arguably the case with Dwight Eisenhower. He demonstrated a remarkable natural ability as a leader, helping the various Allies to work together for one common cause. During his two terms as president, he confronted the Soviet Union as part of the Cold War, ended the Korean War and began the American space program.

Eisenhower was born on October 14, 1890, in Denison Texas, son of David Jacob Eisenhower and Ida Elizabeth Stover. He was their only child. Eisenhower could trace his family roots in the United States as far back as 1741, when his Mennonite family immigrated to the American colonies. The family initially settled in the Pennsylvania Dutch community of Lancaster and then in Kansas. Two years after Eisenhower was born, his parents moved the family back to Abilene, Kansas, where his father made a living as a college-educated engineer. Eisenhower was originally named David Dwight but everybody called him Dwight.

Even though his family were pacifists by religion, Eisenhower showed an interest in the military. After graduating from Abilene High School in 1909, he applied for and was accepted into the U.S. Military Academy at West Point, New York. Eisenhower was not a top student, but he made an impression as an athlete and a leader.

His college football career ended, however,
when he injured his knee trying to tackle
the famous Jim Thorpe.

Eisenhower graduated from West Point in 1915. Supposedly, his name was officially flipped to Dwight David while he was in school. A year after graduating, he married Mamie Geneva Doud of Denver, Colorado. They had two sons: Doud Dwight Eisenhower who died tragically in childhood, and John Sheldon David Doud Eisenhower, who would go on to serve in World War II and would later become U.S. ambassador to Belgium.

Eisenhower was on the move in the years after graduation. He initially served with the infantry and was eventually promoted to third in command of the new Army tank corps during World War I (attaining the rank of lieutenant colonel). He was made a major after the war and served at Camp Meade, Maryland, until 1922. It was here that Eisenhower would become convinced of the importance of tank warfare in future combat.

In 1924, Eisenhower was transferred to the Panama Canal Zone, where he was executive officer to General Fox Conner. Conner helped Eisenhower expand his knowledge of war strategy and tactics. During the prewar years of the 1920s and 1930s, Eisenhower's career went nowhere fast. He served as an aide to General Douglas MacArthur (where he learned how to deal with large egos) and was demoted to lieutenant colonel in 1936. Eisenhower returned to the United States in 1939 and worked in several lackluster staff positions in Washington, D.C. A big break came when he was appointed chief of staff to the commander of the 3rd Army in Texas and was promoted to brigadier general in 1941. Eisenhower had made a name as a talented administrator, but at that point had never held an active command.

After the United States entered World War II, Eisenhower returned to the General Staff in Washington, where he helped draw battle plans against the Japanese and Germans. In 1942, he was appointed Commanding General, European Theater of Operations, based in London. He was later made Supreme Commander of the

Allied forces fighting in Africa and Italy. Finally, in 1943, Eisenhower was made Supreme Allied Commander in Europe, charged with drafting a plan to invade the Continent and defeat Germany. He was promoted to general of the Army (equivalent to the rank of field marshal).

He was able to work with the egos of Omar Bradley, George Patton, Winston Churchill, Field Marshal Montgomery and Charles de Gaulle. The Allies invaded Europe on June 6, 1944, and by May 1945, had defeated the German armies and entered Berlin as triumphant victors. After the German surrender, Eisenhower was named military governor of the U.S. Occupation Zone.

Eisenhower returned to the United States and served as the chief of staff of the Army and later Supreme Commander of the North Atlantic Treaty Organization (NATO). He officially retired from active service in 1952 and was president of Columbia University until 1953.

Based on his heroic status, the Republican Party sought out Eisenhower as a candidate for president in the 1952 election. He agreed, and won the nomination. In a campaign stressing conservative domestic policies and vigilance against communism, he easily defeated Adlai Stevenson, winning re-election in 1956– again against Adlai Stevenson.

Eisenhower's foreign policy did not result in a major thaw in the Cold War. The Korean War ground to a stalemate. Even with the death of Stalin, Eisenhower could make little progress toward any detente with the Soviet Union. Although Eisenhower refused to rescue French colonial forces in Vietnam, he did support the division of the country into a south region allied with the United States and a communist north. He sent a few hundred advisers to the region to help the South Vietnamese armed forces.

Domestically, Eisenhower was more successful. He created the interstate highway system (in part to help with transporting troops in case of war). He maintained and, in some cases, expanded the existing New Deal programs and supported the growing civil rights movement. After the Soviets launched Sputnik, Eisenhower pushed hard to create a viable American space program.

Eisenhower left office in January 1961 and retired to a working farm near Gettysburg, Pennsylvania. He remained somewhat active in politics and promoted the candidacy of Barry Goldwater for president.

The war hero and two-term president succumbed to congestive heart failure and died on March 28, 1969, at Walter Reed Army Hospital. He was buried alongside his parents in a small chapel at the Eisenhower Presidential Library in Abilene.

The Legacy of the Man

Dwight Eisenhower is considered one of the heroes of World War II, but his record as a president is more complicated. After the inauguration of the dynamic John F. Kennedy, Eisenhower seemed to be a dull symbol of the 1950s. He was labelled the do-nothing president because critics felt he had basically let the country run itself. He was also seen as a reluctant supporter of the civil rights movement.

However, Eisenhower's reputation began to rise again in the latter part of the 20th century, based on his wartime leadership, his support of the civil rights movement in Arkansas, his ability to balance the federal budget and a prolonged period of peace during his administration. Many historians now include Eisenhower in the list of top ten presidents.

Eisenhower's name is associated with the interstate highway system, and many institutions and schools are named after him. His image was on the dollar coin from 1971 to 1979, and the second Navy supercarrier was named the USS Dwight D. Eisenhower in his honor.

The Resources

You can read more about Eisenhower's background, his war years and his legacy as president at *www.dwightdeisenhower.com*.

Many books have been written by and about Eisenhower the war hero and the president, including *Eisenhower*, Simon and Schuster, 1991; *Crusade in Europe*, Johns Hopkins University Press, 1997; *Eisenhower: A Soldier's Life*, Owl Books, 2003; *Waging Peace: The White House Years, A Personal Account*, Doubleday & Co., 1965; and *Past Forgetting: My Love Affair With Dwight D. Eisenhower*, Simon and Schuster, 1997.

Mahandas Karamchand Gandhi, *Political Leader*

Who He Is

While it may come as a surprise to many, Gandhi (as he is called) was neither the father of Indian nationalism nor particularly politically influential in the early days of the independence movement. On the contrary: well educated and a lawyer, he was very English in his Indian ways. And he used his time in England, a country that he considered to be the center of modern civilization at the time, to study more than the law. More, as he experimented with English ways, he also became a citizen of the world.

In fact, the great Gandhi was not radicalized until he moved to South Africa and tried to practice law amid the extremes of apartheid and white supremacy. Once he returned to India, he became an advocate of nonviolence and noncooperation, and almost immediately had the opportunity to implement those ideals when he began to play center stage in the political and economic life of India and the Raj. In his autobiography, *The Story of My Experiments with Truth*, *(50 plus one Great Books You Should Have Read*, Encouragement Press, 2006*)* he clearly states his position on nonviolence: "There are many causes I am prepared to die for but no causes I am prepared to kill for."

What Made the Man

Born in 1869 in a rural area of India untouched by foreign intervention, he was taught by his mother the Hindu doctrine of ahisma (to do good, not harm). This belief may have been the kernel around which his ideas about nonviolence grew, and was undoubtedly at the heart of his many nonviolent acts in the face of oppression. As was customary at the time, he was married at a very early age (13) to Kasturba Makhanji, and together they had four sons.

Interestingly, Gandhi was a lackluster student; he
barely made it into the University of Bombay.

His university career seems also to have been uninspired, with the exception of his
excitement about going to London to study for the bar–even though it seems that
he did not want to be a barrister! Nevertheless, after receiving a law degree from
University College, London, he returned to India and attempted unsuccessfully to
set up a law practice in Bombay. His failures continued–he was turned down for a
part-time teaching position–but ultimately he was able to find a job drafting legal
petitions for litigants at court. At this point in his life, no one could have guessed
that he had the stuff of greatness in him. However, a great transformation was just
around the corner.

In 1893, he was retained by an Indian firm with offices in Durban, South Africa,
and moved to South Africa. His experiences there shaped his future. Horrified
by the blatant disregard for the civil and political rights of Indians, he actively
struggled against the oppression by demanding basic rights for them. He stayed
in South Africa until 1914, all the while suffering personal and professional
humiliation at the hands of the legal establishment and the general white
community, which had complete contempt for blacks and Indians. What galvanized
Gandhi the most, it seems, was an effort to deny Indians in South Africa the right
to vote by the Natal Assembly. While unable to affect the end result, his and others'
efforts did bring attention to the political and social plight of Indians, and in 1894
he organized the Natal Indian Congress.

Following the Boer War, harsher restrictions were placed on nonwhites in
South Africa. By 1906, Gandhi was supporting a resistance movement on the
part of Indians against the government. It was here that the first direct use of
nonviolence was advocated. This resulted in his being imprisoned many times. The
teachings of Christ, the writings of Henry David Thoreau (especially his essay *Civil
Disobedience (50 plus one Great Books You Should Have Read*, Encouragement
Press, 2006)) and the Russian novelist Leo Tolstoy strongly influenced him. As a
result of his efforts, the South African government recognized Indian marriages
and eliminated an Indian poll tax in 1914.

But it was not until he returned home to India that he began to develop renown
and stature. It began when he became involved in the Indian resistance and
independence movement in Bihar. There he helped organize poor farmers to resist
British agricultural policy, including a heavy tax that was imposed even during
years of famine. His reputation spread throughout India, especially after the

famous Amritsar massacre of civilians by British troops–his response was to call for nonviolence in the face of violence and noncooperation in the face of brutal retaliation.

Now active in the leadership of the Indian National Congress, he advocated the boycott of British goods, urging Indians to wear homespun, rather than foreign-made cloth. Eventually arrested and jailed, one of his greatest concerns was the growing split in the Congress between Hindus and Moslems (a problem never fully resolved, though greater India was later split into the states of India and Pakistan). As religious violence increased, he embarked upon his famous 3-week fast as an attempt to force reconciliation. The effort was a failure, despite his reputation.

Independence did not bring joy or celebration, but anxiety and utter frustration at partition and religious strife. Gandhi would not support his own Congress Party's acceptance of the conditions for independence (and partition). In fact, after independence, Gandhi again resorted to another maneuver that brought him near death when he protested the partition of the country and took a stand on the terrible religious rioting that was wracking the entire country. It was a great and terrible irony that Gandhi, a man of absolute peace and total dedication to religious principles, should be assassinated on January 30, 1948.

The Legacy of the Man

In his influential autobiography, *The Story of My Experiments with Truth,* Gandhi covered more than 50 years of his life from childhood to adulthood. Although his fights against racism, colonialism and violence established his reputation internationally, the underlying reason for his actions was often overlooked. A very religious man, he attributed his successes to the will of God. He was inspired by a desire to grow closer to God through the purity of his deeds–that is, his simple living, vegetarian diet, celibacy, and ahimsa. Gandhi, who had been subject to much pain in his life, found many answers in Hinduism. "Hinduism as I know it entirely satisfies my soul, fills my whole being." Each chapter of his autobiography reveals important lessons that he felt brought him a little closer to truth and his need to purge himself of the demons within himself. "What I want to achieve–what I have been striving and pining to achieve these thirty years–is self-realization, to see God face to face, to attain moksha (salvation). I live and move and have my being in pursuit of this goal."

His legacy is one of peace, cooperation, charity and piety. In the years since his death, dozens of political and social movements have been based on or have otherwise adapted his principles and concepts, including the American civil rights movement of the 1960s. He is the model of human integrity amidst the chaos, violence and materialism of modern society.

The Resources

No source about Gandhi is better than what the man himself wrote–*An Autobiography: The Story of My Experiments With Truth*, Beacon Press, 1993. The 1982 movie *Gandhi*, starring Ben Kingsley and directed by Richard Attenborough, was well received at the time of its release and is generally considered an accurate and inspiring account of his life.

19

Bill Gates,
Businessman

Who He Is

What is it like to be the richest man in the world, a man whose wealth at one point exceeded $100 billion, according to Forbes magazine? And what is it like to give a huge portion of this wealth to charities and good works the world over? Bill Gates, perhaps the capitalist's capitalist, founded a company that revolutionized every aspect of business, education, communication and entertainment, yet maintains a relatively low profile considering his personal and business success.

There are some, including the European Union and a number of state attorneys general, who would say Gates and Microsoft are monopolists and control too much of the personal computer and Internet world. Further, there are those who would complain that Gates was late coming to philanthropy–not really understanding or willing to take an active, charitable role until his wife Melinda brought him around during a trip to Africa.

However he is viewed–admired or not–he is still a hero to millions, because he made information and technology available for a relatively low price. He is a master of business acumen, inspiring tens of thousands to form their own companies and to attempt to take technology and computing to new levels of sophistication and service.

What Made the Man

This is not a rags-to-riches, but a riches-to-riches story. Bill Gates comes from a wealthy Seattle family, his father a prominent attorney and his mother a bank board member. There is one story, hard to verify, that Gates' father set up a million dollar trust fund for him the year he was born. Gates at various times has denied this story; however, he certainly cannot deny that he had the best in private education, including 3 years at Harvard.

> He never graduated, instead choosing to go into business with
> Paul Allen and others to form a company devoted to software
> development. The year 1975 was indeed a very good year.

Gates and his associates developed a BASIC software for a company called Altair; from this point on, there was no looking back. A big concern to Gates and Allen was that much of the software that was available–used by amateurs and others–was open sourced, meaning that it was produced and distributed for free. Gates objected to this and to the random pirating of his work. He called for a closed source approach to software, meaning that the work and end product were intellectual products that had monetary value. If you want his version of BASIC, you should pay for it. (This very theme continues to haunt software developers, movie producers, singing artists and publishers, and it has become increasingly easy and popular to take from the Internet or other sources rather than pay for the content.)

The real bonanza lay just ahead: a relationship with IBM. At the time, most operating software was written for a particular platform or machine. If you created a new computer, you had to write software specifically for that machine. Using licensed software, Gates and Allen delivered to IBM an operating system for their first major microcomputer. But the real stroke of genius came when Gates realized that the IBM system would be just the first of dozens of competitors; rather than limit his business relationship to IBM, Microsoft was willing to license its MS-DOS (Microsoft Disk Operating System) to a variety of computer manufacturers–at that time and in the years that followed, there were many such manufacturers, though most did not survive.

Gates, and Microsoft's success in operating systems would be challenged by a new breed of developers who came up with the graphical user interface–a system particularly successful at Apple, which became the standard in the industry. Compared to DOS, the resulting Windows was a user's delight, although early versions were subpar when compared to Apple and others. But, as is always the case with Gates, Microsoft did not sit back, but came out with repeated improvements and, of course, all those licenses to the various manufacturers, which ensured installation in millions of computers each year.

Gates, while less and less involved in the day-to-day operations of Microsoft, continues to lead the company to new frontiers, including playstations, Internet-enabling software and plans to compete with the fabulously popular iPod from Apple.

The Legacy of the Man

How will the world remember our hero Bill Gates? Until recently, we would have thought of him as a captain of industry, ranked with Ford, Rockefeller and Carnegie. We would have thought of him as dynamic, rich and famously creative as he expanded Microsoft's reach into the worlds of computing and the Internet. But we would not have thought of him as a generous, giving man.

Much of Gates' current fame must be shared with his wife, Melinda. It is her awareness and her social concern that have prodded the man to participate fully in the modern world. Perhaps it was their combined efforts that attracted Warren Buffett to make much of his huge fortune available through the Bill and Melinda Gates Foundation.

While much is to be said for his and his foundation's efforts, there are some who point out that he lives in a fabulously expensive and expansive house outside Seattle, and that he is one of the most influential people in contemporary America. There are those who credit his wealth and influence to vicious, almost ruthless business practices (a pattern that was long ago set by Rockefeller and others, who cleaned up their reputations with huge grants of money to charity and the arts).

Certainly a great deal of praise was heaped on Gates when he created his foundation in 2000 with an initial gift of $106 million (small peanuts, many said at the time, considering the overall wealth of the man). Subsequent funding has increased rapidly, as has Gates' fame and reputation. The foundation emphasizes scholarships to minorities, AIDS prevention and efforts to eradicate such diseases as polio, diphtheria, measles and yellow fever–diseases that have been controlled in the Western world for many years.

The foundation has grown to over $26 billion and must give away at least 5 percent of its assets each year in order to continue as a charitable organization. (This amount does not include the recent announcement by Warren Buffett that he would give most of his accumulated wealth to the foundation.)

The foundation and his charitable works will ensure that Bill Gates will long be remembered for something more than his aggressive business tactics and great wealth.

The Resources

To learn more about the Bill and Melinda Gates Foundation, visit *www.gatesfoundation.org* for a complete profile of the foundation and its charitable works.

There are many books about Gates, Microsoft and the Bill and Melinda Gates Foundation. *Bill Gates*, Lerner Publications, 2005, is one of the most recent. Visit *www.barnesandnoble.com* for additional information.

20

John Glenn,
Astronaut & Statesman

Who He Is

For several generations, John Glenn was the senior senator from the state of Ohio–known for his traditional Democratic views, more liberal than middle of the road. He spent a long time in the Senate and was a permanent fixture there until his retirement. But, of course, he is not a hero for being a senator–sadly, there are far too few senators anyone would consider heroes.

He is a hero because he was a pioneer in the new field of jet airplanes and space missions. What was it about a man that he would let himself be strapped into an experimental jet airplane and test it at two or three times the speed of sound? What is the internal mechanism that drives a man to want–to fight–to be hurled from the face of Earth as part of the exploration of space?

In many ways, he is no different than earlier explorers who risked their lives and fortunes to do something that no one had ever attempted before. He is our hero because he was driven to repeat history and explore where few had gone before. He is our hero because he came back alive each time and made us feel special about what he had accomplished. And he was our hero because he gave us great pride in our country and its space endeavors.

What Made the Man

In many ways, John Herschel Glenn Jr., was the all-American man. He was born in 1921 in Cambridge, Ohio, and grew up in Cambridge and New Concord, Ohio. He wrote that his childhood was everything a boy could dream of and he flourished as a student.

After receiving a Bachelor of Science degree in engineering from Muskingum College, Glenn decided to enter the military. This was during the early years of World War II, and Glenn was attracted to military aviation. He enrolled in the Naval

Aviation Program in 1942 and was later assigned to the Marines' VMO-155 group in 1944. Glenn flew bombing missions over the Marshall Islands in the Pacific later in the war, and by the time the war ended, had been promoted to captain and stationed at the Naval Air Station Patuxent River. By then he had married his childhood sweetheart, Anna Margaret Castor. He would later have two children with her.

Glenn was a flight instructor in the late 1940s, but he longed to get back into combat, this time in the burgeoning Korean War. He finally got his wish and went to Korea as part of Marine Corps squadron VMF-311. An interesting bit of trivia is that Glenn's frequent wingman during this time was baseball all-star Ted Williams.

After Glenn flew in an interservice program, he shot down three MiGs while flying an Air Force F-86 Sabre and was decorated for this.

The next step toward being an astronaut was Glenn's acceptance into the test pilot school after the Korean War. Although he flew many significant test flights, his early claim to fame was completing the first supersonic transcontinental flight. When he flew over his hometown, the resulting sonic boom had a neighbor running to Glenn's house shouting,

"Johnny dropped a bomb on us!"

Around this time, the United States was scrambling to match the USSR in the space race. The Soviets had already orbited a satellite called Sputnik and sent animals into orbit. They would shortly send Yuri Gagarin into orbit as the first man to enter space. The new National Aeronautics and Space Administration, or NASA, was desperate to catch up, and from hundreds of applicants chose seven test pilots as the Mercury astronauts. This group included John Glenn.

After suborbital flights by Alan Shepard and Gus Grissom, Glenn blasted off on February 20, 1962, aboard the Friendship 7 for America's first manned orbital mission. His flight was not without problems. A malfunction of the automatic attitude control of the capsule forced Glenn to use manual thrusters to maintain a proper position, making him possibly the first man actually to fly in space. A more significant problem that cut the mission short after only three orbits involved a loose heat shield. The shield was designed to prevent the capsule from burning up by the intense heat of re-entry into Earth's atmosphere. NASA ground controllers, afraid that the shield would fall off during re-entry, told Glenn to keep the retrorocket thruster pack attached below the heat shield, in the hope that the belts securing the pack would hold the shield on. The maneuver worked, and John Glenn splashed down to become a national hero.

A few weeks after the assassination of President John F. Kennedy, Glenn resigned from NASA and entered the business world. He was also interested in running for elected office in Ohio and started exploring the possibility of running against Ohio incumbent, U.S. Senator Stephen M. Young. A household injury forced Glenn to pull out of the race. He lost a primary battle in 1970, but won the primary and the general election for U.S. Senate in 1974.

Glenn served with honor in the Senate and was the chief author of the 1978 Nonproliferation Act. He ran unsuccessfully for the Democratic nomination for president in 1984. However, his record was stained when he was included as part of the Keating Five after accepting a $200,000 contribution from a man partly responsible for the savings and loan collapses of the late 1980s. Glenn was exonerated and was found only to have exercised poor judgment. He repeatedly won re-election, finally retiring from politics in 1999.

In 1998, Glenn returned to space as a controversial part of the space shuttle Discovery STS-95 mission. Glenn was there ostensibly to help NASA see how space travel would affect the elderly, but many critics saw it as a publicity stunt. The public loved it, however, and gave Glenn and the rest of the crew a ticker-tape parade, making him one of the few individuals to be the recipient of two ticker-tape parades.

The Legacy of the Man

John Glenn remains one of America's most beloved heroes. He was most famously portrayed by Ed Harris in the film *The Right Stuff*.

Besides his personal achievements, Glenn has lent his name to the NASA John H. Glenn Research Center at Lewis Field in Cleveland, Ohio. The highway running by the Wright-Patterson Air Force Base and Wright State University near Dayton, Ohio, is named the Colonel Glenn Highway.

After leaving elected office, Glenn helped create the John Glenn Institute for Public Service and Public Policy–later to be called the John Glenn School of Public Affairs at Ohio State University–where he still works as an adjunct professor of political science to further the institute's efforts to promote working in public service.

No matter his current activities, Glenn will live on as a dedicated public servant and daring space traveler who overcame mechanical problems with his spaceship to return safely to Earth and maintain NASA's steady progress in landing a man on the moon before the end of the 1960s.

The Legacy of The Astronauts and Scientists of Manned Space Flight

While John Glenn is presented in detail as one of our modern heroes, it goes without saying that he represents not only himself but everyone who was and is involved in manned space flight. The heroes, both Russian and American, are largely unknown–literally tens of thousands of individuals have contributed to what is now one of the most spectacular and heroic ventures that the world has ever seen or experienced. They include the scientists, engineers, researchers, planners and technicians–everyone that was involved and continues to be involved in manned space flight. The face to this massive effort, of course, is the astronauts themselves–many hugely famous throughout the world, including such names as John Glenn, Yuri Gagarin, Neil Armstrong and Buzz Aldren.

In some ways the efforts by these heroes parallel the age of exploration whereby Europeans left in tiny boats to find a route to the Indies, making names like Columbus, Magellan, Hudson, DeGama and a dozen more the stock lore of our history books. The manned flight left one world to venture to something beyond the everyday and ordinary, at great risk and great peril. They were motivated by adventure, by curiosity, by fame, by nationalism and by a sincere desire to expand the ordinary and everyday horizons known in the 20th century.

Contrary to popular belief, the origins of this huge undertaking were long before most readers were alive. The Chinese centuries before had invented gun powder and used it for military rockets and for fireworks. Thousands of years have passed since then with little substantial development. To bring the matter to recent memory, Robert Goddard and others were working on rockets in their earliest and most primitive form in the 1920s and 1930s, launching the first liquid-fueled rocket in March of 1926. Much of his early work was under contract with the U.S. Army, which eventually severed ties with Goddard, thinking his work had no practical value.

In a seminal work around this time, Goddard predicted that a rocket could be launched to the moon (nothing was said about it returning). Scorn was heaped upon Goddard and his associates by the national media–only to print a very inconvenient retraction years later–the day after the launch of Apollo 11. In the end, it was all made right when the Goddard Space Flight Center was established in 1959.

While Goddard was one of the public figures in the United States, tremendous resources and scientific talent were devoted to rocket and propulsion in Germany; the most famous name associated with this kind of research was Wernher von Braun, the developer of the infamous V-2 rockets which terrorized London during the final days of World War II. Historians are hard-pressed to be sure whether, given enough time, the Germans could have perfected rocket science to the point that real, sophisticated weapons could have been developed and that given even more time, their expertise could have been used to develop a manned space program.

In the end, von Braun came to the United States and became the chief designer and developer of the Saturn V launch vehicle which sent the U.S. to the moon. (The stories of his surrender to the American and his attempts to have all or most of his staff and records moved to U.S.–controlled areas are in themselves fascinating reading!) Ironically, he is considered the father of the U.S. space program–despite a soiled reputation by developing the V-2 rockets that randomly killed thousands in London.

What everyone does agree is that in the final days of World War II there was a mad rush for German scientists–both the Russians and the Americans desperately trying to round up the technical talent behind the V-2 and other innovations in flight and rocketry. While the whole matter was deadly serious, some readers will recall the vintage film noir movies of the 1960s depicting darkened Berlin streets and undercover agents, bribing and killing to capture German scientists. In the end, most would agree that the Russians had a huge advantage in the race for space as they were able to get, if for no other reason because of close proximity, the lion's share of technical and scientific talent. Thus began the famous space race, ultimately replaced decades later with the joint development of the International Space Station.

Von Braun's most important benchmark was the launch of the Jupiter-C rocket and the first satellite for the United States--the now famous Explorer 1. While important as it may be, the real credit for substantial strides in the future manned space program goes to the Russians with the launch of Sputnik--the efforts of the famous Sergei Korolev. He and his team personally assembled the components for the first Sputnik capsule, including the now famous one containing a dog.

As early as 1958, Korolev laid the foundation for manned space flight with a series of tests using dogs--the most important part was the ability to return the capsule to Earth and recover the dogs alive. After substantial testing, the Russians agreed to test the concept of manned flight by launching the now famous Yuri Gagarin and eventually the first woman cosmonaut, Valentina Tereshkova in Vostok 6. One can only imagine the sheer terror of these early flights.

While the vast majority of the people who have actually gone into space through the various manned space flights have been part of the military, in the last several decades, more and more people have come from the civilian ranks, including teachers and scientists, (Who cannot remember where they were the day that the crew of the Challenger was lost forever?) Further, the ranks of the many people involved with the various programs, primarily Russian and American, have been internationalized--thus the space race has been changed to space cooperation. Astronauts, following John Glenn's lead, are being trained from dozens of countries--even civilians are getting into the act, beginning with Dennis Tito who made history as the first space tourist in May of 2001. (He paid $20 million to travel to the International Space Station.)

The Resources

You can find the official biography of John Glenn and related information about his two space missions at *www.nasa.gov.*

The film *The Right Stuff* is an entertaining look at the Mercury program. The book by the same name by Tom Wolfe, Bantam Reissue Press, 1983, is more detailed.

Other good books on Glenn include *John Glenn: A Memoir*, Bantam, 2000; *John Glenn: A Space Biography (Countdown to Space)*, Enslow Publishing, 1998; *Back in Orbit: John Glenn's Return to Space*, Longstreet Press, 1998; and *A Hero Born*, Poet Born Press, 1999.

21

Dame Valerie Jane Goodall,
Primatologist

Who She Is

What would cause someone to spend much of her life in the bush working
for, studying and protecting chimpanzees? Surely most of us would see this as
an unusually committed calling for a woman, even one who had developed a
fascination with primates and with Africa.

But she is our hero precisely because she is so dogged in her pursuit of
knowledge and because of her efforts to protect and study chimps in the wild.
And she is our hero because she is unorthodox, stepping out of the box and using
unusual methods to develop theories of chimp behavior and its relationship to
human behavior.

> She is and always will be the darling of animal lovers who
> have put her on a pedestal for her work, her dedication
> and her personal sacrifices for the good of the world.

What Made the Woman

Thanks to multiple appearances in National Geographic magazine (the most
for any one person) and several television documentaries, Jane Goodall is one
of the most recognizable scientists in the world. Her research into the behavior
of chimpanzees substantially changed the way people viewed the relationship
between humans and primates.

Goodall was born on April 3, 1934, in London, the first child of Mortimer Herbert
Morriss-Goodall and the former Margaret Myfanwe Joseph. She has one younger
sister, Judy. Her parents divorced when Goodall was only eight and the two sisters
stayed with their mother, moving to the seaside city of Bournemouth, England, to
live closer to the children's maternal grandmother and two great aunts.

She quickly demonstrated a burning curiosity about the outdoors and the animals that inhabited her immediate area. Goodall devoured the Tarzan books by Edgar Rice Burroughs and told friends she would be a much better Jane to Tarzan than the character in the books. This fascination with the jungle led her to declare at age 11 that she intended to visit Africa and maybe even live there.

By the late 1950s, Goodall had achieved her dream to travel to Africa, but found her initial work as a secretary to be less than fulfilling. She heard that the famed anthropologist Louis Leakey and his wife, Mary, were digging near where she was residing in Zaire. As part of his fossil research linking humans to apes, Leakey had been planning a major study of the great apes. After meeting Goodall, he hired her to be his secretary and was quickly impressed by her enthusiasm, love of the jungle and ability to absorb information and ideas.

Leakey wanted the person who began the study to bring a fresh, unbiased look at the subject. He asked Goodall to join the project and begin with a study of the chimpanzees in the Gombe National Reserve in Tanzania. The study was funded exclusively by Leakey, who thought the project would last for 10 years. Goodall believed it would take longer. More than 40 years later, she is still conducting research at Gombe.

Goodall had the work habits and instincts of a born naturalist, but she did not have the proper educational background. Leakey realized this would work against her research and sent her back to England where she earned a doctorate in ethology from the University of Cambridge in 1964.

She quickly returned to her work in Gombe, and while there met and married Dutch wildlife photographer Hugo van Lawick. The couple had one son and divorced amicably in 1974. The next year she married Tanzania parliament member Derek Bryceson (who was also a director of the country's national parks). Bryceson died of cancer in 1980 after only 5 years of marriage to Goodall.

Goodall was frustrated in her initial attempts to get near to the chimpanzees; she was not allowed to get any closer than 50 feet. It did not help that she came down with two bouts of malaria in the course of only a few months.

She was finally accepted into a chimpanzee troop when a large male wandered into camp and started stomping his feet and screaming. Goodall realized he was interested in a banana on her camp table, and she quickly started using bananas to make contact with the chimpanzees. She also set up a banana-laden feeding station to lure the chimpanzees, but later believed this altered their natural behavior.

Goodall soon had complete access to the chimpanzees at Gombe, who would let her follow them and greeted her, as they do with each other, with a touch or kiss. Unlike other wildlife researchers, she assigned her subjects names rather than code numbers.

After a few months, Goodall realized she was seeing behavior that had never been noted before, behavior that showed chimpanzees to be highly intelligent, emotional creatures living in complicated social groups. She also discovered that, despite popular beliefs, chimpanzees could use mildly complicated tools and would eat meat, making them omnivores and not vegetarians.

By now Goodall's work was exciting enough to Leakey for him to continue funding the project and send additional supplies. She also attracted the attention of the National Geographic, which began chronicling her work in 1964. This would result in cover stories and a variety of television specials on her discoveries.

Goodall lived almost exclusively in her Gombe compound until 1975. She accumulated a wealth of data that is still being studied. She founded Jane Goodall Institutes in nine countries and lectures constantly on chimpanzee conservation and research, and on eliminating the use of chimpanzees in nonessential research.

The Legacy of the Woman

Jane Goodall will always be associated with bravery and honesty in research. When she made her first excursion to Gombe, many scientists questioned Louis Leakey's judgment in sending a young woman into what could be a dangerous situation. She proved them wrong.

Goodall's work has resulted in her being given numerous professional recognitions and awards. She was named a Dame Commander of the British Empire in 2004. In 2002, Kofi Annan, the secretary-general of the United Nations, named her a United Nations Messenger of Peace. Other awards for Goodall include the Medal of Tanzania, Japan's Kyoto Prize and the Benjamin Franklin Medal in Life Science. She is a member of the advisory board of BBC Wildlife magazines. In 2006, Goodall received the 60th Anniversary Medal of UNESCO and French Legion d'Honneur.

Her fame has resulted in several interesting, and sometimes controversial, appearances in pop culture. The Walt Disney Company honored her with a plaque on The Tree of Life at Walt Disney World's Animal Kingdom theme park (along with a carving of her beloved David Greenberg, the first chimpanzee to approach her).

She appeared as herself in Nickelodeon's animated *The Wild Thornberrys* series and is a character in Irregular Webcomic's *Steve and Jerry* series. In an episode of *The Simpsons,* she was spoofed as a diamond-hoarding slave driver of chimpanzees.

Perhaps her most bizarre association with popular culture was a Gary Larson *The Far Side* cartoon showing two chimpanzees grooming. One finds a human hair on the other and asks if her husband is "doing a little research with that Jane Goodall tramp." The Jane Goodall Institute sent Larson a letter complaining about the cartoon, but these efforts were dropped when Goodall admitted how amused she was by it. After the controversy died down, the cartoon appeared on T-shirts, and all profits from sales of the shirts would benefit the Goodall Institute. Goodall maintained a cordial relationship with Larson and wrote a preface to his *The Far Side Gallery 5* collection, praising his work and its depiction of the similarity of human and animal behavior.

Even though Goodall's unorthodox methods resulted in criticism from the scientific community, her discoveries and courageous methods of research have opened a new understanding of how chimpanzees relate to each other and to humanity.

The Resources

Jane Goodall has authored numerous books on her studies and findings among the chimpanzees of Gombe. Many of her television specials are available on DVD and videocassette. You can find out more about her and the Jane Goodall Institute at *www.janegoodall.org.*

Important books by and about Jane Goodall include *Reason for Hope: A Spiritual Journey,* Warner Books, 2000; *My Life With the Chimpanzees,* Aladdin, 1996; *In the Shadow of Man,* Mariner Books, 2000; *Africa in My Blood: An Autobiography in Letters: The Early Years,* Mariner Books, 2001; *Jane Goodall: The Woman Who Redefined Man,* Houghton Mifflin, 2006; and *Jane Goodall: 40 Years at Gombe,* Stewart, Tabori and Chang, 1999.

22

William Franklin (Billy) Graham, *Minister*

Who He Is

The Protestant tradition in the United States has produced generation after generation of great preachers, but no one is more recognized and loved than Billy Graham. His crusades were the backbone of a religious movement and tradition, international in scope, which made Graham stand out as a moral man in a seemingly immoral and imperfect world.

A very elderly man in the early 21st century, Graham's influence was not to be limited by declining health. Rather, it was almost enhanced, as though this generation must see and hear the last of the great preachers. Although his last mission was supposed to be in 2005, at the time of this writing, Graham is still active in his church and ministry.

What Made the Man

Although now firmly in the camp of the Southern Baptist Convention, Graham's family was originally active in the Presbyterian church in Charlotte, North Carolina. (He was born in 1918 and converted to the Baptist church in 1934 as a result of a revival meeting–a frequent event in towns and cities in the South and Midwest.) After high school, Graham attended what is now called Trinity College of Florida and was ordained a minister in 1939. He did further studies at Wheaton College in Illinois, graduating from that prestigious university in 1943.

His real mission in life began just after he graduated from Wheaton, when Graham joined a youth ministry, call the Youth of Christ, and began a series of missions across the United States. Many of these were planned only for a day or two, perhaps a week at the most.

On this grand tour, Graham inspired and awed his audiences. His mission in New York was given nightly and lasted for nearly 16 weeks!

His tours were international, first in English-speaking countries like England and Australia, but eventually in highly restricted places, such as Eastern Europe, North Korea, South Africa and the Soviet Union. Most of his success owed itself to an excellent background and a wonderful stage presence; he came across as an enthusiastic and sincerely religious man. His career, if it can be called that, was certainly helped when Henry Luce, publisher of Time, put his picture on the cover of the magazine. William Randolph Hearst, newspaper mogul, pressured his editors to write about Graham. Many wags would say that their motivation was hardly religious: They wanted Graham to represent the conservative, anti-communist viewpoints that they so strongly held. (Ironically, while not proved, it seems that Graham was a lifelong Democrat.)

This grueling schedule, plus his responsibilities as a writer, teacher, administrator and fundraiser, makes Graham's career all the more remarkable. He is said to have preached in over 180 countries, to some 200 million people throughout his remarkable career—not including hundreds of radio and television broadcasts. What is truly the sign of a hero is that, at age 86 and afflicted with Parkinson's disease, he organized his last crusade in Flushing, New York. However, because of Hurricane Katrina, he chose to add one more stop: New Orleans. For 2 days he preached at what was called the Festival of Hope to tens of thousands in the ravaged city.

The high-profile life often leads to a high-profile lifestyle, as was clear when some prominent preachers (such as the Bakers) became so infatuated with material success that they lost their way in life (and in some cases ended up in prison). For all his time in the public spotlight and for all his exposure and the attention given to his crusades, there is absolutely no evidence that Graham, his son or even his grandson ever exceeded reasonable expectations in terms of salary and compensations. From the beginning to the end of his preaching career, Graham was always a just and good man who put God's works ahead of his personal ambitions and for that he is our hero.

Graham has been the adviser to presidents and other prominent men and women. There is no evidence that he ever used those positions of confidence to push a particular agenda, to enhance his mission or to use his influence in any inappropriate way—other than in helping to seek truth through the Bible.

But, alas, our hero is not without controversy. Someone in the public view for so long cannot help but inspire some contentious sentiments. One of the standing views is that Graham expressed views that were anti-Semitic–or, at least, critical of Jews and their influence on American life. Once exposed, Graham immediately apologized for these comments. However, despite the attempt to right the ship, there has always been a lingering suspicion that the anti-Semitism was more than a casual one-time event.

Another controversial aspect of his life is the amount of time he spent with his fellow co-religionists. Graham was extremely close to the leaders of the Roman Catholic Church, particularly Pope John Paul II–himself a strong advocate of ecumenism and communication with other branches of Christianity. Further, he did not wait for his children to become adults before baptizing them, contrary to the tradition of the Southern Baptist Convention, which believes that children cannot and should not be baptized. Baptism is seen as an acceptance of Jesus, and something that only adults can fully understand and appreciate.

All in all, however, it is fair to say that controversy has been a fairly minor part of Graham's life and ministry, and that it has tended to revolve around smaller, parochial matters rather than any of the outward religious, financial or political scandals that have beset organized religion and some other preachers and pastors.

The Legacy of the Man

By all evidence, Billy Graham is a man of God, which is just as he intended to be. Part of his legacy was to use his fame and considerable skill in the pulpit to draw huge crowds to rallies and bring people forward to conversion. He organized and practiced on a huge scale. His direct, personal appeal to conversion and to prayer were highly effective, though some might say that they were also rather staged–much like an amusement event or a rock concert. Nevertheless, through his preaching, television and radio performances, books, seminars and media savvy, he has influenced four generations worldwide and made us better for it.

He has been awarded the Congressional Gold Medal and Ronald Reagan Presidential Freedom Award, honored by Jews (somewhat ironically) and Christians alike and recognized by various civil rights organizations for his good works and benefits to humanity. His work continues through his son and grandson, although no one can ever pretend to take the place of the original genius that is Billy Graham. He has been and will continue to be the standard for mainstream Protestantism worldwide. He is our hero because he is a virtuous man who dedicated his life to others.

The Resources

Learn more about Graham, his ministry and his mission, by visiting *www. billygraham.org.* Readers will find a host of resources, including a complete listing of his books, of which his first, *Peace With God*, was a national best-seller.

Some very interesting archives are stored electronically in Wheaton College's Website. Visit *www.wheaton.edu* and search under Billy Graham for more information.

23

James Maury Henson,
Entertainer

Who He Is

Who could make us laugh so hard using an entertainment medium so old and so conventional that it was almost absurd? Who could possibly put life in the Cookie Monster or Miss Piggy so convincingly that we found them nearly human in their emotions and behavior? Who could take two names from the classic movie *It's a Wonderful Life*, and use them to such perfection: Bert and Ernie, silly and lovable.

Who could do all this? Jim Henson could. He was a creative and entertaining genius who lived his life through his puppets. He certainly was not the first to use puppets as part of a television act, but he was the first to do it so brilliantly. Through his association with *Sesame Street*, he taught our children the alphabet and how to be safe and how to enjoy learning each morning on public television.

> Like many of our heroes, he lives on through his creations–movies, books, television shows and the characters themselves.

What Made the Man

Besides creating creatures and special effects for fantasy television shows and movies, Jim Henson will always be most closely associated with the Muppets and *Sesame Street*. Such characters as Kermit the Frog, Miss Piggy, Fozzie Bear, Bert and Ernie, Elmo, Oscar the Grouch and Cookie Monster were created, operated and often voiced by Henson.

Henson was born on September 24, 1936, in Greenville, Mississippi. When Henson was 10, his family moved to the Washington, D.C., suburb of Hyattsville, Maryland. Henson was now able to spend more time with his maternal grandmother, who lived nearby. She taught Henson how to do needlework and got him interested in sculpture. Both of these would be valuable skills when Henson began his work with puppets. She is also credited with encouraging his emerging imagination.

While in high school, Henson began a lifelong fascination with puppetry and how it could be portrayed in a revolutionary way on the new medium of television. He believed that the TV camera, by focusing on just the puppet's upper half, would allow much more freedom of movement than a traditional puppet stage. He took these ideas with him when he was hired—with his brother Paul—to create and manipulate the puppets for a children's show on WTOP-TV. He began attending the University of Maryland to study commercial art, but always found himself returning to his love of puppetry.

After a few months in college, Henson would create the first Muppets (the term is a combination of marionette and puppet) for a 5-minute children's show called *Sam and Friends* on WRC-TV. The show was momentous for Henson for two reasons: Jane Nebel, a performing partner on the show would become his wife in 1959 and, in 1955, a primitive version of what would become Kermit the Frog made his first on-air appearance.

Kermit would be a revolution in puppetry. Henson created the head out of softer, more malleable materials that allowed for a far greater range of expression. He perfected his techniques of using the camera frame to mask the puppet operator for a greater range of movement. Henson also created a style of movement for the puppets that involved having the operator use one hand to manipulate the upper body, head and mouth and the other hand to operate the character's arm with a wire from below. The result was something nobody had seen before.

The small local show soon drew the attention of national variety shows hungry for new forms of entertainment. Henson's brand of irreverent, often violent, slapstick and the novelty of the Muppet operation was just what they were looking for, and while in college he was bringing Kermit and company to programs like *The Tonight Show*, *The Steve Allen Show* and *The Ed Sullivan Show*.

Henson rightly sensed that he had created something with tremendous potential. With his wife and new collaborator Jerry Juhl (who would work with Henson for decades), he relocated to New York City in 1963 and founded Muppets, Inc. Soon after setting up shop, Henson created the character of Rowlf, a wisecracking, piano-playing dog, as a regular character on the popular *Jimmy Dean Show*. During these early days, Henson also hired Frank Oz, who would voice some of the most famous Muppets, direct films and feature as Yoda in the *Star Wars* series.

Henson stretched his wings into experimental filmmaking. His short film, *Time Piece*, was nominated in 1966 for an Academy Award for Live Action Short. Even more significant during this period was Henson's involvement in a revolutionary new PBS show for children called *Sesame Street*. Henson's *Sesame Street* characters debuted in 1970.

The Muppets were part of the first season *Saturday Night Live* cast, but did not last very long on the show. The upside to this setback was that producer Sir Lew Grade decided to take a chance on creating a half-hour variety show centering on existing and new Muppet characters. Each show would feature a guest star. Enthusiasm for the show grew quickly among adults and children who loved its irreverent humor. Soon, A-list celebrities were lining up to appear on the show.

Henson was now free to expand into film and made the hit *The Muppet Movie* in 1979. It was followed, in Henson's lifetime, by two sequels: *The Great Muppet Caper* and *The Muppets Take Manhattan*. Henson's creations also graced the fantasy films *Labyrinth*, *The Dark Crystal* and *The Witches*. Other projects included the HBO series *Fraggle Rock* and an animated television show *Muppet Babies*.

In 1990, Henson contracted what he thought was some form of flu. It turned out to be pneumonia caused by a rare and extremely aggressive type of bacteria. By the time Henson finally went to a hospital, the pneumonia would not respond to antibiotics, and he died at the age of 53.

Henson's son, Brian, took over the Muppets and made more movies and television shows. In 2004, he and the other Henson heirs sold the Muppet characters (except for the Sesame Street characters) to the Walt Disney Company. The Jim Henson Company still operates the Creature Shop and controls the rights to its film and television work.

The Legacy of the Man

By almost all accounts, everyone who knew him thought Jim Henson was a terrific man to work with. He encouraged taking chances, was always there to help one of his staff through a problem and was able to clearly communicate his vision to his collaborators.

Unlike many entertainers associated with children's television, Henson never talked down to his audience. He also recognized the importance of keeping adults entertained as well, and used sly humor, a fast pace, wacky slapstick and current references to delight audiences of all ages. Many of the catchphrases from the Muppet characters have entered the popular vernacular.

If Henson had one downside, it was his tendency to push himself in what, some believed, were too many projects at once. This habit of overworking might have led to his pneumonia. His reluctance to stop work and go to the hospital could have been a contributing factor in his untimely death.

However, what most people will remember about Henson is their first glimpse of a Muppet in action and the sheer joy and wonder it could generate. Our hero treated kids as adults and adults as kids, and the world loved him for it.

The Resources

All the Muppet movies are available on either DVD or videocassette. Compilations of *The Muppet Show* are also available on video, as are collections of *Sesame Street,* including the Muppet inhabitants. Songs from the Muppet movies and from *Sesame Street* are available on CD or audiocassette. Information on all things Muppetish and on the legacy of Jim Henson can be accessed through the official Muppet Website at *http://muppets.go.com.*

Books on Henson and the Muppets include *Jim Henson: The Works, the Art, the Magic, the Imagination*, David McKay, 1993; *It's Not Easy Being Green: And Other Things to Consider,* Hyperion, 2005; *Jim Henson: Puppeteer and Filmmaker*, Ferguson Publishing Company, 2006; *Jim Henson's Designs and Doodles: A Muppet Sketchbook*, Harry N. Abrams, 2004; and *No Strings Attached: The Inside Story of Jim Henson's Creature Shop*, Macmilllan General Reference, 1997.

24

Steven Jobs,
Entrepreneur

Who He Is

Steve Jobs is a hero because he and his associates made personal computing
a reality. Yes, he is a very rich man and yes, we tend to favor those who are
successful and wealthy–but there is more to Steve Jobs than that. He is the
quintessential self-made man–someone who rises above his station in life, who has
insight into something new and different–and, most importantly, takes a chance.

He is our hero because he is also the ultimate entrepreneur. Starting a computer
company was not enough for him; he saw the newest technology could be used in
a range of applications and introduced the world to an array of visual delights.

What Made the Man

Very few people in private industry can claim that their creations changed the
world, but Steve Jobs could. Jobs, along with Steve Wozniak, created the first truly
personal computer in the Apple I and Apple II. The new machines made people
rethink what a computer was and what it could do for them. Later, Apple would
release the phenomenally successful Macintosh computer that further expanded
the capabilities and ease of use of a personal computer.

Jobs was an orphan adopted by Paul and Clara Jobs of Mountain View, California,
on February 24, 1955. He did not like the schools at Mountain View, and his
parents decided to move to Los Altos, California, so Jobs could attend Homestead
High School. He was described, at the time, as something of a loner and as a
student who was always willing to take a fresh look at problem solving.

Jobs started attending lectures at the Hewlett-Packard campus in Palo Alto,
California. He was eventually hired as a summer employee and met the man who
would change his life–Steven Wozniak, who was regarded as an engineering whiz
kid who loved to invent gadgets. One of those inventions was the infamous blue
box, an illegal pocket-sized telephone attachment that allowed users to make long-

distance phone calls for free. Jobs, the emerging businessman, helped Wozniak sell these devices.

After graduating from high school in 1972, Jobs started attending Reed College in Portland, Oregon, but stayed there only for one semester. Even though he was not an official student, he hung around the campus for another year, taking philosophy classes and immersing himself in the early 1970s counterculture.

During the next few years, Jobs drifted. He took a short-term job as a video game designer at Atari in 1974, then left that to travel to India in search of spiritual enlightenment. When Jobs returned to California, he got back into contact with Wozniak, who had started the Homebrew Computer Club, which encouraged creating a computer that could be easily used by a large number of people. Unlike Wozniak, who loved creating electronic products, Jobs was more interested in the marketability of those products.

He conceived the idea of a personal computer and persuaded Wozniak to provide the technical expertise.

The Apple I computer was initially designed in Jobs' bedroom and built in his garage. The initial reaction to the product was positive, and Jobs and Wozniak sold everything they could to raise operating capital to market the new computers. Jobs came up with the company name, Apple, because it reminded him of a happy summer he had spent as an orchard worker in Oregon.

Jobs and Wozniak began marketing the Apple I in 1976, selling it at a fairly reasonable price of $666. The Apple I was the first single-board computer with a built-in video interface and on-board ROM, allowing it to load programs from an external source. The first computer was designed primarily for computer enthusiasts.

For the general consumer, Jobs and Wozniak created the Apple II. The design varied little from the Apple I, but it quickly built up a reputation as the Volkswagen of personal computing, thanks to its ease-of-use and durability. Jobs brought in professional marketers and money from venture capitalists, and within 3 years of its creation, the Apple II had earnings of almost $140 million. The company went public in 1980 and Jobs and Wozniak found themselves instant millionaires.

Apple started facing a serious challenge from IBM's new line of personal computers and Jobs realized he would have to market computers that could be used in the business environment that IBM dominated. After stumbling with the Apple III and the Lisa (the first personal computer to be controlled with a mouse), Jobs hit pay dirt with the Macintosh in 1984. The computer used a unique interface that allowed users simply to point and click with the mouse to operate the computer, rather than having to type in MS-DOS commands. The new computer was still not compatible with IBM, so Jobs had to try to market it on its own merits. One of the most successful of those was the Macintosh's ability to do desktop design and publishing. Jobs also worked hard to portray Macintosh users as young, informal and still living a counterculture life.

Just as sales of the Macintosh were soaring, an internal revolt at Apple resulted in the board of directors stripping Jobs of most of his responsibilities. Jobs felt he had been forced out of the very company he had worked so hard to create. Soon, Jobs had no say in how the company was operated. He took his money and left.

Jobs spent some time bicycling and traveling, but felt lost. In September 1985, after meeting with Nobel laureate Paul Berg, Jobs came up with the idea of creating computers that would benefit higher education. Jobs officially resigned from Apple and took five employees with him for his new venture. Jobs created NexT to build hardware and software for object-oriented computers. The efforts failed at first, and Jobs is still struggling to create new software at NexT, concentrating on reference material.

Meanwhile, Jobs had married Laurene Powell in 1991 and had three children with her (he also has a daughter, Lisa Brennan-Jobs with Christine Brennan, whom he never married).

NexT was bought by Apple in 1996, and Jobs returned to the first company he had created. Jobs was made interim CEO and immediately canceled several Apple projects. He used the NeXTSTEP software to create the Mac OSX operating system. In 1998, Jobs introduced the iMac, an all-in-one personal computer with a unique and charming design.

Jobs would enter the entertainment industry in 1986 when he bought Lucasfilm's computer graphics division, renaming it Pixar. After a series of successful short films, Pixar released the first full-length computer-animated feature *Toy Story*, distributed by Walt Disney. The success of that film and its followers made Pixar a superstar. Disney and Pixar could not negotiate a new contract in 2003-2004, and Jobs said that Pixar would find a new partner. However, Robert Iger, the new CEO of Disney, patched up relations and bought Pixar in 2005. Jobs became the largest single shareholder in Disney with 7 percent of its stock.

The Legacy of the Man

Steve Jobs will always be considered an amazingly successful entrepreneur who made money by providing a valuable product at a reasonable price. His management style was aggressive and demanding and not for everyone's taste, but it was well suited to the wild days of PC development in the 1980s.

His work with Pixar has created some of the best-loved animated features in recent history, and he is still pursuing new technologies in hardware and software for Apple and Pixar. Still only in his early 50s, it is likely Jobs will conquer other worlds before he is ready to retire.

Jobs certainly made his share of mistakes and erroneous assumptions as he developed his businesses, and his management style resulted in the burnout of many key employees, but he was still a true visionary who saw a way to substantially improve people's lives and make a lot of money doing it.

The Resources

More information on Steve Jobs, Apple and Pixar can be found at *www.apple.com* and *www.pixar.com*.

Jobs has been the subject of several unauthorized biographies and has yet to write an autobiography. Books about him include *The Second Coming of Steve Jobs*, Broadway, 2001; *Apple Confidential 2.0: The Definitive History of the World's Most Colorful Company*, No Starch Press, 2004; *Steve Jobs: The Journey Is the Reward*, Lynx Books, 1988; and *Steve Jobs and the Next Big Thing*, Scribner's, 1993.

25

John Paul II,
Pope

Who He Is

In a century of seemingly declining interest in organized religion, how does a Roman Catholic pope become an international hero? John Paul II is literally worshipped in his homeland, Poland, as a national icon. He is adored worldwide by young people whom he took a particular delight in visiting and for whom he said mass at various Catholic youth rallies through the decades. Here is a man who aged before our eyes because of Parkinson's disease, yet whose moral authority would help bring down what Ronald Reagan called the evil empire–the Soviet Union.

John Paul II was not a church reformer. He did not embrace new theologies or modern interpretations of Catholic theology and tradition. On the contrary, he was an avowed conservative who considered church tradition and teachings unaffected by the world or its changing appetite for organized religion. He stood face to face with radical political leaders in Central America, an overwhelmingly Catholic part of the world, and criticized their Marxist social ideology. He was unafraid and undeterred by criticism that he and his church were outdated and outmoded.

Yet despite all the contradictions, the world largely grieved when this pope died. Almost immediately, efforts began to have Pope John Paul II canonized as a Catholic saint. What was it about his personal charm and religious zeal that made him so popular and so important in people's lives?

What Made the Man

John Paul II was born as Karol Jozef Wojtyta in the southern Polish town of Wadowice in 1920. While his mother died at an early age, his father worked hard to keep his young son in school. Throughout school and university, Karol was a good athlete–even as pope, it is reported that he went skiing and was physically active.

His university studies were interrupted by World War II–the university faculty was arrested and the facility closed. Everyone had to get a job, and Karol did just that. While institutions of higher learning failed to function, the bishop of Krakow was sponsoring an underground seminary that Wojtyta attended, eventually being ordained a priest in 1946. Because the young man had promise, he was sent to Rome to study at the Pontifical University. He would go on to earn two degrees in theology (the equivalent of our Ph.D.), and in both cases had difficulties securing the actual degree. Nevertheless, he clearly was popular, bright (he spoke at least 10 languages) and upwardly mobile in the Catholic Church in Poland. By 1958, he was a bishop and was the cardinal of Krakow by 1967.

An odd turn of events would bring Wojtyta to the head of the Roman Catholic Church. In 1978, Pope John Paul I was elected pope at age 65. However, he was in poor health and died some 30 days later. This meant that another pope had to be elected.

Wojtyta was a compromise candidate for two popular and promising Italian cardinals–after all, the church had not elected a non-Italian as pope since the 16th century and there never had been a Polish pope ever in the history of the papacy!

At 58, he was one of the youngest men to take the ring of St. Peter. His papacy would continue for 26 years, one of the longest in modern times. During that time, he would travel to over 100 countries and was active–politically, socially and religiously–throughout the world, combating a variety of isms: particularly communism, but also fascism, unrestrained capitalism, materialism, imperialism and racism–just to mention a few.

This pope was no pushover; he knew what he wanted, and it was not a church mired in controversy or new theology. He was a traditionalist, and seemed out of step with many in Europe and North America–except for the young people whom he admired and loved. These young people returned that devotion. He was a Catholic's Catholic, extending the influence and teachings of the church and not at all afraid to lecture presidents and prime ministers. He detested war and was very concerned for the emerging church in the Third World.

This pope was famed for his opposition to communism and his efforts to free Poland from Soviet influence. He was a staunch supporter of personal freedom and defiantly opposed those who would restrict it, to the point that some theorists conjecture that it was his opposition to communism that induced attempts on his life. Because he traveled so widely, he was extremely open to, and made every effort to improve relations with, Judaism, the Orthodox Church, Muslims and other non-Christians.

There were only two things that tried to slow this pope down: an assassin's bullet and the onset of Parkinson's disease. Pope John Paul survived the assassin but did not survive the effects of a progressive disease. The first indication of Parkinson's disease appeared as early as 1992. The contrast between the older and younger man was pronounced. The entire world watched and suffered as the disease slowly deprived the pope of his mobility and his voice.

By the time of his death, many were already calling him Pope John Paul the Great, in reference to the expected efforts to have him canonized as a saint of the church and in recognition of his religious teachings and his striving to improve the conditions of peoples everywhere.

The Legacy of the Man

John Paul II was a man of extraordinary energy, talent and genuine warmth. While considered by most to be holy man, a man of integrity, there are those who found him controversial. He was famous for making apologies for errors of the past. However, to many it seemed that he was unable to see some of the church's most obvious contemporary failings.

He viewed himself as a pacifist, and saw little justification for war of any kind. He was very early in his condemnation of the U.S. invasion of Iraq and in the use of force anywhere. There are those who saw his conservative stances concerning sex, women in the church, the use of contraception, abortion and same-sex marriage as not in keeping with the times and actually contributing to the AIDS and overpopulation problems, among others.

Perhaps one of the most controversial charges against this pope was that he reacted too slowly to the sexual abuse charges against priests in the United States and elsewhere. He seemed very reluctant to take firm action, according to some critics.

In addition, because he lived a long life and was in poor health for his last several years, some felt that he should have stepped down as pope in favor of a younger, healthier man.

So how shall we think about this pope and his legacy? Certainly, he has one of the finest reputations of any world leader, religious or not, in the 20th century. Millions came to see him, greet him and hear his masses and sermons as he traveled around the world. He was not shy in chastising leaders of the great powers for their indifference to the suffering of the Third World and certainly was willing to take a stand on any issue for which he felt there was a compelling moral issue. Yet he was theologically and socially stubborn, affirming traditional church teachings and practices.

The Resources

The official record of Pope John Paul II can be found on the Vatican Website. Visit *www.vatican.va* and search the database for more information and details about his life and work. In addition, visit *www.pbs.org* and search the huge collection of archives and videos for insights, interviews and video clips on the life of John Paul II.

To really understand the man and his vision, the best approach is to read his writings directly. Consider reading *Pope John Paul II: In My Own Words*, Gramercy, 2002. The book is available from most online booksellers; visit *www.amazon.com* or *www.barnesandnoble.com* for more information.

26

Michael Jordan, *Athlete*

Who He Is

There is something about this great athlete that simply overwhelms people, to the extent that they want to be like Mike. Surely Michael Jordan, a man who captured the attention of sports fans everywhere, is the sports hero of the 20th century.

Who else could have done what Jordan did? Who else could have brought a so-so team like the Chicago Bulls to national prominence with championships year after year? What was it about him that caused us to flock to stores to buy shoes named after him? Why was–why is–his presence so appealing all over the world?

What Made the Man

Jordan is considered by most to be the greatest player in the history of the game. During his career, he was named an All-Star 14 times and led his team to two separate National Basketball Association (NBA) championship three-peats. He has also been credited with gaining global recognition for the league.

Michael Jeffrey Jordan was born on February 17, 1963, in Brooklyn, New York, the third son of James and Delores Jordan. He grew up in Wilmington, North Carolina. As a child, his greatest love was baseball, a passion that he shared with his father. However, Jordan started playing one-on-one pickup games against his older brother, Larry, and basketball soon moved into the No. 1 spot in his heart.

Jordan attended Emsley A. Laney High School. He was suspended various times during his freshman year. He was cut from varsity basketball the following season due to an underdeveloped 5-foot-11-inch physique. However, he eventually became an excellent student and a star on the baseball, basketball and football teams. He finally made the varsity basketball team, averaging 25 points per game in both his junior and senior seasons. As a senior, Jordan was selected for the McDonald's All-American team and became the only high school player in history to average a triple-double with averages of 29.2 points, 11.6 rebounds and 10.1 assists.

After his super senior season, Jordan played for the University of North Carolina Tar Heels on a basketball scholarship. In 1982, he played somewhat below the radar as a freshman underneath upperclassmen stars James Worthy and Sam Perkins, but stepped into the spotlight at the end of the year during the NCAA championship game against the Georgetown Hoyas and his future NBA rival, Patrick Ewing. With seconds left, he carried the Tar Heels to a 63-62 victory.

He was named the College Player of the Year by The Sporting News in 1983 and 1984, and received the Naismith and Wooden awards in 1984. The summer after his junior year, Jordan led the U.S. Men's Basketball Team, coached by Bobby Knight, to an Olympic gold medal in Los Angeles. Then, in the 1984 NBA draft, he was selected as the third overall pick by the Chicago Bulls. He left school after that, but eventually graduated from North Carolina with a Bachelor of Arts degree in 1986.

Jordan married Juanita Vanoy in September of 1989. The couple live in the Chicago area with their daughter and two sons.

The Legacy of the Man

The Bulls had won only 28 games in their last pre-Jordan season. In his first NBA game, on October 26, 1984, he scored 16 points against the Washington Bullets, before scoring 40 or more points seven times and finishing his rookie season as one of the top scorers in the league with an average of 28.2 points per game.

Jordan, nicknamed Air Jordan established himself as one of the finest players in the league during his second season in the NBA, scoring 50 or more points eight times during the regular season. He joined fellow legend Wilt Chamberlain to become one of only two players to score 3,000 points in a single season.

Jordan carried the Bulls into the playoffs every year, but the team did not make it all the way to the NBA finals until the 1990-1991 season. The year before, the Bulls faced the Detroit Pistons in the Eastern Conference Finals and the Pistons employed what had become their usual game plan against Jordan's team: the Jordan Rules. Basically, they tried to force Jordan out of commission by double- and triple-teaming him every time he got the ball, stopping him from going to the baseline and hacking him whenever he drove to the basket. Jordan agreed to an offensive change by Coach Phil Jackson and Assistant Coach Tex Winter.

The Bulls began playing with a triangle offense and finished in first place for the first time in 16 years, reaching a franchise-record 61 wins in a single regular season. Jordan and his team went on to win their first NBA championship ever in 1991 against Magic Johnson and the Los Angeles Lakers. The Bulls went on to defeat Clyde Drexler and the Portland Trailblazers in 1992 and Charles Barkley and the Phoenix Suns in 1993.

In 1992, Jordan went to the summer Olympics again,
this time as a member of the original Dream Team,
which was the first Olympic team to include NBA players
on its roster. Jordan averaged 12.7 points per game in
Barcelona and won his second Olympic gold medal as the
team swept through with a 6-0 record.

In October of 1993, Jordan announced he was going to retire. It was speculated that there were two main reasons for his early first retirement. One was that his father had been tragically killed by armed robbers in July of that same year. The other was that the NBA had started an investigation into allegations that Jordan had illegally bet on league games, though all accusations against him were later cleared.

After retiring from the NBA, Jordan signed a minor league contract with the Chicago White Sox. He played as an outfielder for the Birmingham Barons, a White Sox farm team. Masses of fans flocked to watch Jordan play his new game, but his batting was nowhere near as good as his shooting. After 127 games with the Barons, he finished with a .202 batting average.

Even though the Bulls had retired his number, 23, he announced his return to the team on March 18, 1995, with probably the shortest ever press release, which stated simply, "I'm back." The very next day, he put on his new jersey number, 45, to finish out the rest of the regular season with the Bulls. They eventually lost to the Orlando Magic in that year's Eastern Conference semifinals.

Jordan began wearing his old number, 23, on a mission to prove that he was even better than before. In the 1995-1996 season, he led the Bulls to finish 72-10, the best regular season record in the history of the NBA. He also topped the league in scoring with 30.4 points per game and carried his team all the way to their fourth NBA championship victory against the Seattle SuperSonics. Jordan and the Bulls continued to dominate the league for the next 2 seasons.

Jordan retired from the NBA for a second time on January 13, 1999. He became president of Basketball Operations and part owner of the Washington Wizards. After the team won a measly 19 games in the 2000-2001 season, a disappointed yet motivated Jordan started training again, eventually signing a 2-year contract with the Wizards. After the devastating attacks of September 11, he announced that he would donate his entire season's salary to victims and their families. Jordan retired for a third and final time after his last game on April 16, 2003.

The Legacy of the Man

Jordan has become one of the most marketed and widely recognized athletes in history. His face first popped up on a Wheaties cereal box in 1988, and he has worked as an influential spokesperson for such companies as Nike, Gatorade, Hanes, Nestlé, McDonald's, Ball Park Franks, MCI and Rayovac. Nike developed a shoe in his honor, called the Air Jordan.

Jordan has also done his fair share of charity work. He remains an advocate of The Boys and Girls Clubs of America. Jordan, along with the Bulls franchise, built the James R. Jordan Boys and Girls Club and Family Life Center in 1996 to honor the memory of his father and to serve Chicago's West Side community. He also established the Jordan Family Institute at the University of North Carolina, and has been involved with America's Promise, the United Negro College Fund, the Make-A-Wish Foundation and the Special Olympics.

The Resources

To learn more about Michael Jordan visit the following Websites:

www.23jordan.com.
www.virtualfans.com.

For a revealing take on the pro basketball career of Air Jordan, read:

The Jordan Rules, Simon & Schuster, 1992.
Driven from Within, Atria, 2006
When Nothing Else Matters: Michael Jordan's Last Comeback,
    Simon & Schuster, 2005

27

Martin Luther King, Jr.,
Civil Rights Activist

Who He Is

Entire generations have seen, and future generations will continue to see, the famous speech delivered in Washington during the height of the civil rights movement, *I Have a Dream*. Here stands the inspiring image of a man who had devoted his entire life to improving the rights of African-Americans, not only in the South but also the segregated cities of the North.

First and foremost a pastor and a religious leader, he gained prominence as a persistent, nonviolent revolutionary whose sole mission in life was to change society's understanding of what was right and legal and reasonable. How, he asked, could an entire segment of the United States be relegated to second- or third-class status? How was it possible, 100 years after the Civil War, that blacks had less freedom and equality? Why was it that the religious and political leaders in the United States did not do something about this? Well, it was his mission to do something about it, regardless of the cost or sacrifices.

What Made the Man

Martin Luther King Jr. was born a preacher's son in Atlanta, Georgia, in January of 1929. He would follow his father's footsteps, first taking a degree at Morehouse College, a traditionally all-black school, and then ultimately a Ph.D. from Boston University. Interestingly, historians and others have looked back at King's writing and a great deal of concern has been expressed about plagiarism in King's dissertation work. The controversy was so great that the university did an analysis of the dissertation and concluded that a substantial portion was taken from other students' efforts. Perhaps greatness–in this case a Nobel Peace Prize–allows for another standard: Boston University decided not to revoke the degree even though there was ample evidence for them to do so.

King began his formal tenure as a Baptist pastor in 1953 in Montgomery, Alabama, and used the church and its pulpit to launch his formal entry into the existing civil rights movement. (King did not start the movement; rather, attempts to get blacks equality with whites had been going on since the end of the Civil War.)

The essential elements of King's leadership style surfaced very early: nonviolence (as practiced by Gandhi and A. J. Muste) and the power and influence of the media. King intuitively understood that using force against the existing political and social structure would be futile and only inflame the situation. He understood the importance of image, as presented by the media. If blacks, striving for their rights, were the aggressors, they would gain little sympathy from the rest of America. Further, he knew that the image of innocent and passive people, abused and beaten by the police in full view of the cameras, would have a tremendous psychological effect.

One of the first opportunities to practice these combined principles came with the Rosa Parks incident and the Montgomery bus boycott of 1956. For more than a year, citizens refused to ride the buses, and downtown merchants lost a tremendous amount of business as a result. Tensions were so great that King's house was bombed and he was put in prison (not the first time and certainly not the last). The boycott was a huge success, however, resulting in national recognition of the problems of segregation in the South and of King's new prominence in the movement.

It is a testament to King and the civil rights movement
that it provoked even the U.S. Supreme Court into action
when it outlawed segregation on public transportation.
This was the first of many court decisions on civil rights that
changed the face of American society forever.

The creation of the Southern Christian Leadership Conference (SCLC) is the enduring legacy of King. He founded the organization to channel the combined power, moral and otherwise, of the predominately black Baptist churches throughout the South. The SCLC was hardly the only organization working for civil rights, and there were huge differences among them on the use or nonuse of violence as a means to an end.

Two particularly noteworthy campaigns are the marches led by King to Washington and Chicago. The demonstration in Washington was controversial before it began. President Kennedy and others used their influence to tone down the demonstration—basically to make it less critical of the role of the federal government in the civil rights movement. No matter the original intent, the demonstration was ultimately a huge success, culminating in the famous speech, I *Have a Dream*.

The march into Chicago was a dirty little affair; the leaders of SCLC were shocked to see how people lived in the slums of the big cities. Further, the rancor was worse than any southern protests that the demonstrators had encountered to date. The reaction by whites in Chicago was extreme and the enthusiasm of the city's politicians can be described as tepid at best.

In 1965, King announced his opposition to the Vietnam War. Because he was early in his opposition, he lost support from middle-class groups and organizations that found his view too radical. Vietnam was merely a subset of the larger criticism he leveled against the American government, corporations and the general moral tone of the day. From his critics' point of view, civil rights were only part of this distasteful troublemaker; he was also unpatriotic and un-American.

A fascinating relationship between King and the FBI (and its leader, J. Edgar Hoover) began in 1961-62. In an ever-growing effort to discredit King in any way possible, the FBI used a variety of tactics—accusing him of being a Communist and of having extramarital affairs—to peel away his credibility and his moral authority. There are some who say that King's death at the hand of James Earl Ray in Memphis in 1968 was actually contrived by the FBI. However, the fact remains that he was killed by an assassin and that his work would remain unfinished—or at least that it would remain for others to complete.

The Legacy of the Man

How do we understand this man? He won a Nobel Prize and a national holiday is named for him. He was a religious man with an almost obsessive compulsion to see changes on the local and national levels in terms of race relations and greater openness for African-Americans throughout society. He had a quiet, deliberate and highly motivating personality, capable of using the media and few words to make a highly effective impression on his people and on the country at large. He was ranked in recent polls as one of the top three greatest Americans ever.

Yet he was a man of many messages, a far more complex hero than is immediately apparent. He was not the only leader of the black movement and was often in conflict with other leaders and other organizations because of his unwillingness and inability to change tactics—he would not become violent or more radicalized, no matter how great the injustice.

He found himself the center of great controversy–which many considered a distraction and off message for his primary goal. He advocated reparations to former slaves and their families (an idea which is still current among some black leaders). He took on an increasingly anti-government and anti-business stance, again causing some confusion as to what the real goals of his movement might be.

Although those around him insist that his personal behavior was above reproach, there are persistent rumors of infidelity and the seemingly very real problem of plagiarism in his academic career.

Martin Luther King Jr. gave his life for his cause. He inspired, he challenged, he acted and he led in a way that few men or women the 20th century did. He inspired a new generation of leaders not only to be active in the movement but also to join the established order and make continuous improvements. Most importantly, his legacy is reflected in the fact that the Civil Rights Act of 1964 was passed and became law.

The Resources

A terrific Website with information about the King holiday, excerpts from various speeches, information about his wife, Coretta Scott King, and much more can be found at *www.holidays.net/mlk.*

Information about King's award of the Nobel Peace Prize can be found by visiting the Nobel Foundation's Website at *www.nobelprize.org.* Stanford University, at the request of Mrs. King, has been assembling the papers of Dr. King's life, both primary and secondary sources. For more information about this project, visit *www.stanford.edu/group/King/mlkpapers.*

28

Bruce Jun Fan Lee,
Martial Arts Star

Who He Is

Like Superman, Bruce Lee is our hero because he represents what we think a real hero ought to be–strong, quick, athletic and always the good guy. This is Bruce Lee to the millions who watched his exploits in movies and television. He is, of course, one of our many fantasy heroes, thrilling and entertaining us with amazing physical feats and always triumphing against the bad guys.

He was innovative in that he made the martial arts into a national craze. And he was a tragic hero, dying tragically young, never fulfilling his extraordinary potential. He paved the way for others to fulfill their dreams as a martial arts specialist in mainstream culture. Finally, he always was fun, letting us forget our troubles for an hour or two.

What Made the Man

Bruce Lee brought martial arts films to the mainstream American audience. He championed new styles of martial arts based on his personal philosophy and demonstrated how to develop a strong body.

Lee was Chinese-American, born in San Francisco in 1940 to a Chinese father and Chinese-German mother. They were both performers in the Cantonese Opera Company. He and his family returned to their home in Kowloon, China, when Bruce was only 1 year old.

Lee's Cantonese name Jun Fan means invigorate San Francisco. His American birth doctor gave him the American name Bruce. He would not be referred to as Bruce by his family until he was old enough to enter high school. Further complicating things is that Lee's screen name translated in Cantonese as Lee Little Dragon, a name that was used in Lee's first Cantonese movies.

Lee attended St. Frances Xavier's College from 1957 to 1959. During that time, he got into a fight with a local gangster's son. His father feared for his safety and sent him back to the United States to live with a family friend in San Francisco. Lee would later find his way to Seattle, where he received a diploma from the Edison Technical School. He enrolled at the University of Washington as a philosophy major and met his future wife Linda Emery.

In 1964, Lee and Emery married and had two children, Brandon and Shannon. Lee was restless at school and was eager to develop his own form of martial arts and an accompanying philosophy. He combined several types of martial arts, including Tai Chi Chuan, Hung Gar and Wing Chun (which he learned mostly while living in China) into a new type of martial art called Jun Fan Gung Fu.

The technique relied heavily on Wing Chun, combined with elements of Western-style boxing and fencing. Two of the showiest elements of Lee's martial arts were his two-finger pushups and the one-inch punch. The two-finger pushups used only the thumb and forefinger. The one-inch punch was much more impressive. According to observers, Lee would hold his hand outstretched to about one inch from the chest of his opponent. He would then thrust forward with enough power to send the other fighter flying backward. The technique would often be used in his films.

Lee gained notoriety in the martial arts community when he opened his first schools in Seattle, Oakland and Los Angeles in the early 1960s. After showing his techniques in a series of demonstrations and staged fights, Lee started to believe that his Jun Fan Gung Fu, as well as other martial arts, were too restrictive. He developed a new free-form system called Jeet Kune Do (The Way of the Intercepting Fist), which he taught and was to use in his films.

As part of developing his new martial arts techniques, Lee emphasized a specialized philosophy combining Taoism, Buddhism and Krishnamurti, which taught that staying formless and flexible is important in martial arts and life in general. Lee also developed his own system for physical fitness, putting aside traditional body-building techniques to highlight speed and power. He combined weight training and aerobic work with an emphasis on developing the abdominal muscles (Lee believed all martial arts moves involved the abs). He ate very little meat, used health foods and high-protein drinks and ate a diet rich in fruits and vegetables.

By this time, Lee's undeniable martial arts talents and compelling presence were starting to interest Hollywood, who recognized there was a large and growing audience for films featuring martial arts. Lee's first exposure to the broader

American public was as Kato, the assistant to the title character in *The Green Hornet*, based on the popular comic book. The show ran for only one season from 1966 to 1967, but American audiences became fascinated with Lee.

While Lee made more television and movie appearances, real stardom eluded him. He created the character Caine and the television series, *Kung Fu*, intending to play the title role himself. Instead, producers hired David Carradine for the role.

> Lee was very bitter at what he perceived as a snub of his talents and turned his attention to films co-produced by Hong Kong and American producers.

He would make just five films, but each became more and more popular. He started in 1971 with *Fists of Fury*, which was a big hit, and followed it with *The Chinese Connection* in 1972 (a play on the American hit *The French Connection*), *Return of the Dragon* in 1972, *Enter the Dragon*, released after his death in 1973, and *Game of Death*, also released posthumously in 1979. Chuck Norris, a friend of Lee's and soon to be a martial arts star in his own right, played one of the villains in *Return of the Dragon*.

It appeared that Lee was well on his way to movie superstardom as well as great fame as a martial arts innovator when tragedy struck. In 1973, Lee was in Hong Kong discussing the making of the movie *Game of Death*, when he suddenly complained of a headache. His hostess gave him a prescription analgesic known as equagesic. When Lee did not show up after taking a nap, his host found him unconscious. Lee was transported to the Queen Elizabeth Hospital, where he was declared dead on arrival. Doctors found that Lee's brain had swelled and attributed his death to a cerebral edema. They later ascertained that Lee was allergic to equagesic. Death by misadventure was the final verdict.

Bruce Lee, a model of strength, discipline and physical fitness was only 32.

The Legacy of the Man

More than anyone, Bruce Lee contributed to America's fascination with martial arts in the 1960s and 1970s. His combination of good looks and unbelievable fighting moves had never been seen before. Most performers who have succeeded in martial arts movies in the United States credit their success to the early fame of Lee.

Lee's unexpected death has been the subject of much controversy. Some fans believe he was murdered by Chinese triads seeking protection money or was killed by jealous martial arts teachers or film producers. Despite these conspiracy theories, there has been no hard evidence that Lee died of anything other than unfortunate natural causes.

One can only speculate on what would have happened if Lee had not died at such a young age. His films were gaining in popularity and many believe it was only a matter of time before he starred in a big budget Hollywood martial arts film series. Certainly, other martial arts performers have subsequently enjoyed great success. One example is Jackie Chan, who, as Yuen Lo Known, did stunt work in *Fists of Fury* and played a henchman whom Lee kills in *Enter the Dragon*.

The cloud of tragedy that hung over Bruce Lee extended to his son Brandon. Brandon was beginning a promising career in the movies when he appeared in *The Crow*. He was killed by a faulty blank bullet during filming. Ironically, Lee's character Chen in *Fists of Fury* was killed in a similar way.

The Resources

Bruce Lee's films and a compilation of *The Green Hornet* are available on DVD. After his death, some unscrupulous producers incorporated unused footage from Lee's films to create movies that purportedly starred the martial arts master. Information on Lee, his films and his style of martial arts can be found at *www.allbrucelee.com*.

Books by and about Bruce Lee include *Tao of Jeet Kune Do*, Ohara Publications, 1993; *Bruce Lee's Fighting Method: Volumes One, Two, Three and Four*, Ohara Publications, 1993; *Bruce Lee: The Celebrated Life of the Golden Dragon*, Tuttle Publishing, 2000; and *The Bruce Lee Story*, Ohara Publications, 1989.

29

Charles Lindbergh,
Aviator

Who He Is

Greatness and heroism are often a matter of firsts–first black player in baseball, first great inventor, the first person with a new discovery. Charles Lindbergh was the first to fly nonstop across the Atlantic Ocean in a single-prop airplane.

Like many heroes, Lindbergh had his moments where fame played a cruel hoax on him and his family. His child was kidnapped and the crime became the sensation of the nation. His political and social views became controversial and the grasping public demanded more and more of him. Should one brave, seemingly impossible act have made him a hero for life? Did he corrupt his hero status with his later actions? Perhaps–but there is no denying that at one point, Charles Lindbergh was history and a great modern hero.

What Made the Man

Lindbergh was born on February 4, 1902, in Detroit. He grew up on a small farm near Little Falls, Minnesota. His father, Charles August Lindbergh, was a lawyer and also a U.S. Congressman from 1907 to 1917. His mother was Evangeline Lodge Land, a chemistry teacher.

From childhood, Lindbergh demonstrated extraordinary mechanical ability and enrolled at the University of Wisconsin at the age of 18 to study engineering. However, Lindbergh's real interest was not college, but the rapidly growing field of aviation. In 1922, he left school and joined a mechanics and pilot training program with Nebraska Aircraft.

After this training, Lindbergh purchased his own plane, a World War I era Curtiss J-N4 (or Jenny) and joined the ranks of barnstorming stunt pilots. These pilots (many former combat pilots) attempted to maintain and build interest in aviation by flying around the country and performing risky aerial maneuvers. They also offered airplane rides to the rural spectators. Lindbergh followed his barnstorming years by training with the U.S. Army as an Army Service Reserve Pilot and then becoming a mail pilot. He quickly gained a reputation as being able to deliver the mail in any type of weather.

Lindbergh became interested in pursuing the Orteig Prize. The $25,000 prize would go to any pilot who could fly nonstop from New York to Paris. Eight years after its creation, it still had not been claimed, although some pilots were getting close to winning it.

Lindbergh used his knowledge of mechanics and flying to persuade a group of St. Louis businessmen to finance his quest for the Orteig Prize. His backers gave him the funds to design and manufacture a special plane, made by the Ryan Aeronautical Company of San Diego. He called his new plane the Spirit of St. Louis and tested it in early May 1927 by flying from San Diego to New York City with one overnight stop in St. Louis. This flight set a transcontinental record.

He was now ready to take on the challenge of winning the Orteig Prize. Lindbergh took off from the Roosevelt Airfield in Nassau County, Long Island, on May 20, 1927. His flight took a little over 33 hours and led to him landing successfully at Le Bourget Field, near Paris, on May 21 at 10:21 p.m. He was awarded the French Legion of Honor and the U.S. Army's Distinguished Flying Cross, and was celebrated in a ticker tape parade down Fifth Avenue in New York City. At this time, he gained his two nicknames: Lucky Lindy and the Lone Eagle.

After his achievement, Lindbergh wooed Anne Morrow, the daughter of U.S. diplomat Dwight Morrow. She was reportedly the only woman the shy aviator had ever asked on a date. She shared his love of flying and became a pilot herself. She would join Lindbergh on later exploratory flights and would also gain recognition as a poet and writer.

Lindbergh and his wife would have six children. The most tragically famous of them would be their oldest son, Charles Augustus Lindbergh III. Shortly before his second birthday, Charles was kidnapped from the Lindbergh home. The child would be found dead in a nearby field about 10 weeks later. Police charged a carpenter, Bruno Richard Hauptmann, with the kidnapping. His trial would become a media circus. Although many observers thought that the intellectually challenged Hauptmann was being railroaded, he was convicted of the crime and executed for it in 1936.

The tragedy and media attention forced the Lindberghs to move to Europe to maintain their privacy. While he was there, he was invited by the governments of France and Nazi Germany to inspect their aircraft facilities. He was especially impressed by German aviation technology. While in Germany, he was awarded a German Medal of Honor by Nazi official Hermann Goering. Lindbergh's acceptance of the medal would cause an outcry in the United States and led to later questions about his Nazi sympathies.

Lindbergh and his family returned to the United States in 1939. In 1941, he joined the America First Committee, an organization that was actively opposing U.S. entry into World War II. Lindbergh's stature made him a leading spokesperson for the cause of isolationism and he would go on to claim publicly that British, Jewish and pro-Roosevelt groups were leading the country into a disastrous conflict. Some believed Lindbergh stepped over the bounds from political comment to anti-Semitism. His criticism of Roosevelt led the president to publicly denounce him. Lindbergh resigned his commission in the Army.

The isolationist movement in the United States faded after Pearl Harbor and the country entered the conflict. Lindbergh tried to return to active service but was refused based on his earlier speeches against Roosevelt and the war. He still served the war effort by being an aviation adviser to the Ford Motor Company and was in the Pacific war arena as a civilian adviser to the U.S. Navy. He flew almost 50 combat missions.

Following World War II, Lindbergh essentially withdrew from the public spotlight. He served for a time as a consultant to the U.S. Air Force when Dwight Eisenhower was president. Eisenhower restored Lindbergh's commission and made him a brigadier general in the Air Force in 1954. Lindbergh later worked with Pan American World Airways and helped design the Boeing 747 jet. One of his last public appearances was to give his regards to the crew of Apollo 8, the first spacecraft to ever leave Earth orbit in 1968.

Lindbergh developed an interest in conservation and traveled the world to look at how technology and the ecology could work in harmony. He eventually settled in Maui, Hawaii, where he died of cancer in 1974. He was buried on the grounds of the Palapala Ho'omau Church in Maui with this marker inscription: If I take the wings of the morning, and dwell in the uttermost parts of the sea.

The Legacy of the Man

Lindbergh's political controversies unfortunately took attention away from the very real contributions he made to aviation. Based on his flights (often with his wife), Lindbergh developed methods of charting polar air routes, flying at high altitudes and increasing fuel-consumption rates. After his historic flight, he designed a watch for Longines to make navigation easier for pilots. The watch is still being used.

Motivated by the debilitating heart condition of his sister-in-law in the 1930s, Lindbergh helped design an artificial heart. The device was still many years from being perfected, but at the time it worked amazingly well.

However, Lindbergh is still viewed critically by many who question his sympathies prior to the U.S. entry into World War II. One of the most recent of these is the novel by Philip Roth, *The Plot Against America*, which portrays Lindbergh as the president of the United States. In the book, he signs a neutrality pact with the Nazis and begins persecuting U.S. Jews. Others, like political commentator Patrick Buchanan, have claimed that Lindbergh was smeared for views that, at the time, were common.

Politics aside, the vision of the heroic Lone Eagle will probably be most closely associated with Lindbergh who brought the attention of the world to the potential of aviation.

The Resources

Charles Lindbergh was portrayed by Jimmy Stewart in the movie *The Spirit of St. Louis*, which is available on DVD or videocassette. Lindbergh's story of his flight, *The Spirit of St. Louis*, is still a popular book and won a Pulitzer Prize when it was published. More information about Charles Lindbergh can be found at *www.lindberghfoundation.com*.

Other books on Charles Lindbergh and his historic flight include *Lindbergh*, Buckley, 1999; *Charles A. Lindbergh: A Human Hero*, Clarion Books, 1997; *We*, Kessinger Publishing, 2003; and *The Case That Never Dies: The Lindbergh Kidnapping*, Rutgers University Press, 2004.

Nelson Rolihlahla Mandela, *Civil Rights Leader*

Who He Is

Some people are heroes; others fall in the very special category of superheroes. Nelson Mandela is one of our superheroes! Imagine spending 27 years of your life in prison, most of them in one of the most brutal and horrible places in South Africa. People have survived and will continue to survive long years of confinement, but to do so with your values, dignity and principles intact is another story.

While he is lauded by most of the world, it is important to note that Mandela once advocated violence as a means to an end in South Africa. Whether terrorist or hero, there can be no doubt that Mandela emerged as a nation builder—a nation of blacks and whites.

A matter of great significance, often overlooked during Mandela's amazing career, is that he ensured a transition from a white-dominated society to an all-inclusive government without further violence or upheaval.

What Made the Man

Mandela was born Rolihlahla Mandela on July 18, 1918, to the Thembu Xhosa family in the village of Mvezo in South Africa's Mththa district. Mandela's father was active in local politics and helped Jongintaba Dalindyebo ascend to the Thembu throne. Mandela became the first member of his family to attend a formal school when he enrolled in a Methodist-run elementary school.

One of the teachers gave Mandela the name Nelson in honor of the British Admiral Horatio Nelson.

When Mandela was nine, his father died of tuberculosis and he was informally adopted by Jongintaba. Mandela continued his education and attended a Wesleyan mission school near the regent's palace and the Clarksbury Boarding Institute, where he studied extensively in Western culture. He received his certificate a year earlier than his peers and attended Healdtown, a Wesleyan college in Fort Beaufort. He then started to study for a B.A. at Fort Hare University where he met Oliver Tambo. The two were destined to be friends and colleagues throughout their tumultuous lives.

Two events led to Mandela traveling to Johannesburg: He was forced to leave college after leading a student boycott of the university's policies and he objected to an impending arranged marriage. He worked several small-time jobs in the city, while completing a correspondence degree from the University of South Africa, and started studying law at the University of Witwatersrund.

Mandela began his political activism with the African National Congress (ANC) shortly after the 1948 election of the pro-apartheid National Party. Apartheid was legal racial segregation, with blacks having little or no rights in a government totally dominated by white South Africans. Mandela was prominent in developing the ANC's Defiance Campaign and the 1955 Congress of the People. The adoption of the Freedom Charter at this congress provided the fundamental blueprint for a nonapartheid country.

Espousing a philosophy of nonviolence, Mandela was arrested and released several times in the 1950s. At the same time, his and Oliver Tambo's positions as leaders of the ANC were being challenged. They tried to bolster their positions by alliances with minority political parties, but these efforts were not well regarded.

Another group called the Pan Africanist Congress (PAC) split away from the ANC and further weakened its influence. Mandela decided to match the PAC's militant stance by now supporting an Israeli-style guerilla campaign of violent resistance to apartheid. In 1961, he co-founded and became the leader of the ANC's armed wing.

After spending some time on the run, Mandela was arrested in 1962. He was finally sentenced to prison in 1964 for advocating sabotage and crimes against the government. He would spend the next 27 years in prison, 18 of them in a brutal facility on Robben Island.

Mandela refused an offer of conditional release in 1985 in return for his denouncing the violence and armed movement of the ANC. He remained in prison until 1990 when overwhelming South African and international pressure led to his release. At the same time, the ban on the ANC was lifted by then President de Klerk.

In 1994, South Africa held its first election in which both blacks and whites could participate. To little surprise, the ANC won the majority and Mandela was installed as the country's first black state president. Frederik de Klerk would serve as deputy president. Mandela was president until 1999, and helped the torn country start to reconcile its racial differences and end the lingering results of apartheid.

Mandela also sought to help other disputing countries resolve their differences. He was instrumental in setting up the structure that would bring suspects in the Libya-sponsored bombing of Pan Am Flight 103 to trial, hoping to use the trial to form closer relationships between Libya, the United Kingdom and the United States.

Mandela separated from his wife Winnie while he was president, later to divorce her in 1996 (he had been married previously in the 1950s to Evelyn Ntoko Mase with whom he had three children). Two years later, on his eightieth birthday, he married Grace Machel, widow of former Mozambique President Samora Machel.

Mandela retired from the presidency in 1999 and entered a new phase of his life as an advocate for several social causes while the world stood in line to heap honors on him. He was diagnosed with prostate cancer and underwent radiation treatment.

Due to declining health and a desire to spend more time with his family, Mandela announced his retirement from public life in 2004 at the age of 85. He still continues to write and occasionally speak on issues important to him, his country and the world at large.

The Legacy of the Man

Nelson Mandela will always be a symbol of courage and forbearance under difficult conditions. He saw an unfair system and tried to help stop it in the face of incredible odds. He was able to use his intelligence and education to articulate strong positions, make logical arguments against the very nature of apartheid and attract the loyalty and devotion of not only a small number of supporters in the ANC, but in his country and the entire world.

It is almost impossible to imagine staying imprisoned for almost three decades and still being able to inspire followers into staying the course. However, this is what Mandela did, and his ultimate reward was his release (untainted by charges that he compromised his principles just to get out of prison) and the presidency of the country. It was an amazing change of fortune.

Mandela's main legacy as president of South Africa is the progress that was made in peaceful relations between the blacks and the Afrikaner-dominated apartheid parties. Instead of calling for reprisals against the white minority, he worked hard with former President F.W. de Klerk to bring the two races together for the common good. This would prove to be a daunting task that is still being struggled with today.

After Mandela's retirement, he was showered with accolades and awards, the highlight being the Nobel Peace Prize in 1993. Other honors he received during this time included the Order of Merit and Order of St. John from British Queen Elizabeth II, the Presidential Medal of Freedom from President George W. Bush and honorary citizenship from Canada (the only living foreigner to be given this).

Mandela has been criticized for shifting his protest focus from nonviolence to guerilla-type warfare, resulting in the deaths of hundreds of blacks and whites. Also, his economic policies have not shown any lasting improvement in black citizens' lifestyles, with many still trapped in violent slums and shantytowns.

One area in which Mandela himself believed that he had failed as president was in drawing attention to and addressing the rapidly growing HIV/AIDS epidemic in his country. After his retirement, he made up for this perceived oversight by participating in AIDS fundraising campaigns and several international AIDS conferences.

Mandela has emerged as a hero, but no hero is perfect. By any standard, however, he showed the courage and perseverance to inspire his people and change his nation forever.

The Resources

Nelson Mandela makes a brief appearance at the end of Spike Lee's biographical movie *Malcolm X*. Several documentaries on his life are available on DVD. You can find information on apartheid, the ANC and the life of Nelson Mandela at *www.anc.org.za*.

Other resources on Mandela include his autobiography *A Long Walk to Freedom*, Back Bay Books, 1995; *In His Own Words, Little*, Brown, 2004; *Nelson Mandela: A Biography*, Griffin, 1999; *Nelson Mandela: The Man and the Movement*, W.W. Norton and Co., 1994; and *Nelson Mandela: No Easy Walk to Freedom*, Scholastic Paperbacks, 1991.

31

John Sidney McCain III, *Senator*

Who He Is

John McCain was our hero in the past–as a prisoner during the Vietnam War–and he is our hero now–as a senator, politician and a conscience for the United States and the world. Few famous military heroes emerged from the Vietnam War, which became hugely unpopular.

Certainly, there are still those who would criticize a man who signed a document denouncing the United States while in captivity in Hanoi. In addition, all our heroes have flaws, and some of McCain's, while obvious, are rather inconsequential in light of his past heroism and his potential as a senator and possible presidential candidate.

We admire John McCain because he has the right stuff and because he demonstrated a bravery and tenacity that few of us could ever muster; and we respect him for his unflinching commitment to his principles, whether we agree with him or not.

What Made the Man

It seemed that John Sidney McCain III was destined for service in the Navy almost from the day he was born, August 29, 1936, in Coco Solo in the United States-controlled Panama Canal Zone. His father and his grandfather were admirals in the U.S. Navy. McCain followed the family legacy by entering the U.S. Naval Academy in 1954. Not an academic star, he finished 895th out of his class of 900.

> He joked later that he was following in the footsteps
> of his father and grandfather, both of whom were
> undistinguished scholars at the academy.

After graduation from the academy, McCain underwent flight training at the Naval Air Station in Pensacola, Florida. His flight training and early service as an aviator were not without mishaps. His training plane crashed into Corpus Christi Bay, though McCain escaped without serious injury. After graduation and his entry into the U.S. Navy's light attack forces, McCain was flying well below the appropriate altitude while on a mission in Spain. His plane clipped an electrical cable. McCain landed safely, but many Spanish homes were blacked out due to the accident. McCain's father was the U.S. Naval Commander in Europe at the time, and many contemporaries believe he stepped in to prevent charges being filed against McCain.

Soon after this incident, McCain was flying to the annual Army-Navy football game when his plane suffered an engine failure and McCain had to eject before the aircraft crashed.

McCain's personal life went through significant changes during this period of growing into the difficult job of being a naval officer. He met and married Carol Shepp, a model, in 1965.

In the late 1960s, McCain was stationed on the aircraft carrier USS Forrestal off the coast of Vietnam. In 1967, he had another near brush with death when a Zuni rocket was accidentally launched by an F-4 Phantom while on the carrier's deck. The rocket hit an A-4E Skyhawk that McCain was preparing for launch. The impact ruptured a fuel tank and the ignition of the plane's jet fuel knocked two bombs loose. McCain was able to escape by jumping from the nose of the plane. Less than 2 minutes later, one of the bombs exploded, killing 134 sailors, destroying other aircraft and causing enough damage to threaten the entire ship. McCain suffered shrapnel wounds in the legs and chest.

Soon after his recovery, McCain volunteered to join the VA-163 Saints stationed on the USS Oriskany. The Saints suffered the highest rate of loss of any Navy flying unit in the Vietnam War.

McCain became one of those statistics when, on October 26, 1967, his A-4 Skyhawk was shot down by a Soviet-built SAM (surface-to-air missile). He crash-landed in the Truc Bach Lake near Hanoi and suffered two broken arms. He was captured by the North Vietnamese who proceeded to strip him of his uniform and torture him by stabbing him in the left foot and groin with a bayonet and crushing his shoulder with a rifle butt.

After McCain was transferred to the infamous Hanoi Hilton facility for U.S. prisoners of war, he was further beaten by his guards (McCain would lose all of his teeth as part of the torture and to this day cannot raise his arms above his head).

The North Vietnamese saw value in McCain because his father was the commander of all U.S. naval forces stationed off Vietnam. His captors offered McCain a chance to go home–a ploy designed to embarrass him, his father and the Navy. However, McCain and his fellow prisoners had long made a pact that no one went home until everybody went home, and he refused to be released. After repeated torture, McCain did agree to sign an anti-American propaganda message, which he still deeply regrets. The North Vietnamese decided they could not use the first message and ordered McCain to sign a second one. This time, he refused and reportedly suffered at least two beatings a week.

As the U.S. involvement in Vietnam wound down in the early 1970s, McCain was released from captivity with other POWs in 1973. He was reinstated to flight status and was made the commander of the East Coast A-7 Corsair training squadron. McCain retired from the Navy in 1981 after being awarded a Silver Star, Bronze Star, Legion of Merit, Purple Heart and Distinguished Flying Cross.

McCain relocated to Phoenix after his retirement from the service. McCain has admitted to having extramarital affairs after his return from Vietnam. He and his first wife divorced in 1980, and soon after he married Cindy Hensley, the chairman of a large Arizona beer distributorship. Cindy Hensley suffered a stroke in 2004, but appears to have made a complete recovery.

Besides these changes in his personal life, McCain was also contemplating entering politics. He won a congressional seat after the retirement of John Jacob Rhodes, and in 1986 succeeded Barry Goldwater as a U.S. Senator from Arizona. McCain soon established himself as a social conservative but fiscal moderate–positions that stamped him as a centrist Republican. This image made him more acceptable to the general electorate (an important consideration, given McCain's presidential ambitions), but alienated more conservative elements in the Republican Party who called him a Republican in name only.

While in the Senate, McCain has fought hard to hold down spending, even voting against military projects. He has been a tireless advocate for a reduction in pork barrel spending and campaign finance reform. In cooperation with Wisconsin Senator Russ Feingold, McCain finally managed to pass significant legislation reforming the current methods of financing political campaigns.

McCain has taken other seemingly conflicting stances on major political issues: For example, he was one of the Gang of 14 moderate Republicans who managed to compromise with Senate Democrats on using a filibuster to block judicial appointments, supporting the war in Iraq and sponsoring legislation for fair treatment of detainees in the war on terror.

In 2000, McCain ran hard for the Republican nomination for president. He had early successes in New Hampshire, but eventually lost the nomination in a bitter fight against future President George W. Bush. Many consider McCain to be the top contender for the wide-open 2008 race for the Republican nomination.

The Legacy of the Man

McCain shies away from being called a war hero, saying a real hero would not have been shot down. But, it is undeniable that this aspect of his background has helped his political career as well as giving him a stubborn streak in his dealings with Congress and members of his own party.

No one doubts McCain's sincerity and his ability to work tirelessly for causes that he believes in, but many political pundits question his judgment regarding public appearances. His penchant for questionable humor and his short fuse have often worked against him. Other detractors point at his tendency to appear on television or in movies that they consider inappropriate. This includes hosting *Saturday Night Live*, making appearances on *The Daily Show* and *The Conan O'Brien Show,* and doing a cameo in the raunchy comedy *The Wedding Crashers*.

However, McCain takes these hits and keeps moving forward on issues he deems important, all the while keeping his focus on the presidential race of 2008.

The Resources

John McCain's experiences as a POW were portrayed in the A&E TV movie *Faith of My Fathers*, airing Memorial Day, 2005. The movie is based on his memoirs by the same name (Random House, 1999).

Other books on John McCain include *John McCain: An American Odyssey*, Fireside, 1999; *Man of the People: The Life of John McCain,* Wiley, 2002; and *Citizen McCain*, Simon and Schuster, 2002.

32

Sandra Day O'Connor,
Supreme Court Justice

Who She Is

She is our hero not just because she was the first woman to sit on the Supreme Court, but as much for her fairness, personal integrity and preoccupation for the preservation of the Constitution and the laws of the land.

She is a living standard of what most people expect from the judiciary: A judge who used her power and influence for the good. A woman with high standards, she resisted political pressure in her efforts to build a coalition on the Supreme Court that was both moderate and politically neutral. She remains a symbol of what a judge and scholar should be.

What Made the Woman

Appointed by President Ronald Reagan in 1981 and serving until her retirement in 2005, Sandra Day O'Connor was the first woman to serve as a justice on the U.S. Supreme Court. She participated in some landmark decisions during her tenure on the court, and quickly built a reputation as an intelligent and open-minded justice.

O'Connor was born on March 26, 1930, to Harry A. Day and Ada Mae Wilkey Day. Although she frequently refers to herself as a Texan, she grew up on the family-owned Lazy B Ranch, near the town of Duncan in southeastern Arizona. The Lazy B took up almost 200,000 acres and ranched more than 2,000 head of cattle. O'Connor helped tend the ranch and referred later to these experiences as helping her to develop a work ethic that led to later success.

She spent almost 8 years by herself on this lonely and remote ranch. Her early childhood companions were her parents, the ranch hands, a pet bobcat and some javelina hogs. She had to learn to entertain herself and did so by burying herself in books. Her mother kept up her informal early education by reading the Wall Street

Journal, Los Angeles Times, New Yorker and Saturday Evening Post. O'Connor also learned how to mend fences, keep up when riding with the ranch's cowboys, fire a .22 rifle and drive the ranch truck.

By age five, O'Connor was spending the school months with her maternal grandmother, Mamie Wilkey, in El Paso. This allowed O'Connor to attend the Radford School, a private institution for girls only. However, her summers brought her back to the family ranch. O'Connor maintained this schedule of spending school months with her grandmother until she was finished with high school, taking 1 year off at age 13 because of a severe bout of homesickness.

O'Connor would say later that her grandmother's strong will and high expectations were a big influence on her life.

O'Connor, a gifted student, graduated from high school when she was only 16. She entered Stanford University in 1946 and received a degree in economics, magna cum laude, in 1950. At this time, women were just starting to make inroads into being attorneys. O'Connor decided to pursue the law and entered Stanford Law School. She worked on the Stanford Law Review and won membership in the prestigious Order of the Coif legal honor society. She graduated third in her class in 1952. The same year, O'Connor married John Jay O'Connor III, whom she had met while working on the law review.

Postgraduation, O'Connor found it difficult to obtain a position with a private law firm. The only job offered to her was as a legal secretary. She decided to try to work in the public sector and was hired as a deputy county attorney in San Mateo, California. She found she enjoyed working in public service and later said this first job had a profound influence on her life and career.

John O'Connor graduated 1 year after his wife and joined the U.S. Army Judge Advocate General Corps. He served with them for 3 years in Frankfurt, Germany. O'Connor joined her husband in Germany and worked as a civilian lawyer for the Quartermaster Corps. After John O'Connor's discharge, the couple returned to the United States and took up residence in Maricopa County, Arizona. They would have three sons over the next 6 years.

O'Connor opened her own law firm (with partner Tom Tobin) after the birth of her first child in 1958. She stopped working and became a full-time mother after the birth of her second son. However, she stayed busy outside the home, doing volunteer work, composing questions for the Arizona bar exam, starting a state bar's lawyer referral service, working with the local zoning commission and serving on the Maricopa County Board of Appeals. In 1965 alone, O'Connor maintained a busy schedule as an administrative assistant at the Arizona State Hospital, an adviser to the Salvation Army and a volunteer working with African-Americans and Hispanics.

During this period, O'Connor became involved in Arizona Republican politics. She returned to full-time employment in 1965 as an assistant state attorney general. O'Connor was appointed to fill the Arizona Senate seat of Isabel A. Burgess in 1969 and would go on to win re-election to two more terms. She was elected majority leader in 1972, the first woman to ever hold such a position in the United States. During this time she established a moderate-to-conservative voting record.

O'Connor won a hard-fought battle to become a state judge on the Maricopa County Superior Court in 1974. She was appointed by the governor to the Arizona Court of Appeals 5 years later. Within 2 years, in 1981, President Reagan nominated her to the U.S. Supreme Court, fulfilling a campaign promise to appoint a woman to the high court. She won Senate confirmation 99-0 and was sworn in on September 26, 1981.

At this point, O'Connor was considered very conservative. This view changed over time, and by 1984 O'Connor was described as a restrained jurist, a strong interpreter of federalism and careful interpreter of the Constitution. Over the next two decades, she would emerge as more of a centrist on the court and was thought to be a swing vote in several close decisions.

During her career on the Supreme Court she would rule on issues of religious freedom, endorsed affirmative action for minorities designed to correct a demonstrated wrong and upheld the court's earlier decisions on abortion. She has also favored restricting federal intrusions on state powers (influenced by her own service as a state senator).

Through it all, O'Connor maintained a reputation as a hard worker. She survived a bout of breast cancer in 1988, and finally decided to retire from the Court, making her announcement on July 1, 2005. Her retirement was delayed when Chief Justice William Rehnquist died soon after her announcement. Her original replacement, John Roberts, was then nominated for chief justice, and eventually Samuel Alito was confirmed to replace her in January 2006.

O'Connor has frequently stated that she planned to spend her retirement traveling and spending time with her family. However, work will always be there, and to date O'Connor has already agreed to serve on an American Bar Association commission to explain the separation of powers and roles of judges to the nation's legislators.

The Legacy of the Woman

Sandra Day O'Connor's most visible legacy was in her groundbreaking role as the first woman to sit on the U.S. Supreme Court (she would be followed by Ruth Bader Ginsburg).

She will also be remembered for her move from strict conservatism to a more open view of the issues. Legal experts say that her opinions are still on the conservative side, but are open-minded and reflect no profound ideology. Critics believe that her opinions lack passion or a lofty vision. She has been described as a justice who looked to resolve each case and no more, one with no overarching philosophy that might preordain a result.

O'Connor's law clerks describe her as very much in control and an intense perfectionist. However, they also say she was warm, down-to-earth (as fits her ranch background) and always upbeat. She often eased the long hours in her office with popcorn, Mexican food or outings to the Smithsonian.

The Resources

You can find more information on Sandra Day O'Connor and the U.S. Supreme Court at *www.supremecourtus.gov*.

Books by and about O'Connor include *Sandra Day O'Connor: How the First Woman on the Supreme Court Became Its Most Influential Justice*, Ecco, 2005; *Lazy B: Growing Up on a Cattle Ranch in the American Southwest*, Random House, 2003; *The Majesty of the Law: Reflections of a Supreme Court Justice*, Random House, 2004; and *Sandra Day O'Connor: Justice in the Balance*, University of New Mexico Press, 2006.

33

Rosa Parks,
Civil Rights Activist

Who She Is

Rosa Parks was no one special–just a hard-working woman who simply was tired and refused to go to the back of the bus. She had had enough of the Jim Crow nonsense and she said so, quietly and defiantly.

She used her moral authority, sense of righteousness and her moral outrage to change a system of social interaction that had been oh-so-carefully maintained for nearly 100 years. What she did was simply say no to the face of authority and power. She spoke volumes with a single action.

She is our hero specifically for saying no, for taking a small stand and showing by example that change could come and that Jim Crow and the whole Southern system of segregation could be challenged.

What Made the Woman

Rosa Parks was born on February 14, 1913, in Tuskegee, Alabama. After her parents separated when Parks was a young child, she stayed with her mother and moved with her to Montgomery, Alabama. Parks grew up as part of an extended family that included her maternal grandparents and her younger brother.

At an early age, Parks was exposed to the overt racism of the Deep South in the 1920s and 1930s. In those days, the South practiced almost total segregation of African-Americans from whites. These segregationist policies were commonly referred to as Jim Crow laws. There were separate schools (usually of inferior quality) for African-Americans, special sections in restaurants for African-Americans (some restaurants served African-Americans from the kitchen door or simply refused any service at all), separate restrooms and even separate drinking fountains.

One aspect of segregation that would later make Parks a nationally known figure was separate seating–at the back, naturally–for African-Americans on the city's public buses.

Despite all these injustices, Parks, with encouragement from her mother, grew up to be a young, proud woman. She married a barber named Raymond Parks when she was 20. They both worked and led a fairly comfortable life. At this time, Parks started to become active in the local chapter of the National Association for the Advancement of Colored People (NAACP) as well as the Montgomery Voters League, a group that helped African-Americans pass the tests that were required at the time to register to vote. Parks began to show her disdain for segregated facilities.

At the time, for Parks and many African-Americans in Montgomery, the most visible and onerous example of segregation was the city's public bus system. Under the system at the time, African-American customers were required to use the front door to enter the bus, pay their fares, then exit back out the front door and re-enter at the rear door.

The first four rows of the bus were designated for whites only. Behind these seats was a middle section African-Americans could use. However, if so much as one white person sat there, all the African-Americans had to leave those seats. Finally, there were the rows in the back exclusively for African-Americans. Despite the fact that African-Americans constituted the vast majority of bus riders, it was not unusual to see them having to stand when there were plenty of empty seats in the whites-only rows or middle section. Understandably, this caused a lot of anger and frustration among the African-American riders.

In 1955, Parks was employed as a seamstress at the Montgomery Fair Department Store. On December 1, she had what she described as a particularly hard day. When she finally got on a bus to go home, all the seats for African-Americans were full and she ended up sitting in the middle section of the bus. When a white customer entered the bus a few stops later, he demanded a seat in the middle section. The driver told Parks and three other African-American riders to move. Parks was the only one to refuse. The driver threatened to call the police. Parks told him to go ahead.

The driver made good on his threat and Parks was arrested, fingerprinted and jailed. Black leaders in Montgomery saw this as an opportunity to challenge the restrictive bus regulations and perhaps deal a fatal blow to the other segregated facilities. Parks agreed to go to court to challenge the law that led to her arrest.

In the meantime, Montgomery African-American activists decided to boycott the entire bus system as of December 5. African-Americans walked, participated in car pools or rode bicycles to get around during the boycott. The city dug in its heels and the boycott ended up lasting 381 days, until a long-standing lawsuit by the NAACP challenging the bus segregation laws finally made it through the courts. Ending up in the U.S. Supreme Court, the justices found for the plaintiffs and outlawed racial segregation on buses, deeming it unconstitutional. The court order went into effect on December 20, 1956, and African-Americans began riding the buses the next day.

The boycott took its toll on Parks and her family. Both she and her husband, Raymond, lost their jobs and the continual harassment she received ended up causing him to suffer a nervous breakdown. In 1957, Parks, Raymond and her mother moved to Detroit, where she worked for a while as a secretary. She was still sought after as a symbol of the developing civil rights movement.

As her reputation grew, Parks was awarded several honorary degrees and eventually worked on the staff of Detroit Congressman John Conyers. Even after she officially retired, she was still a much sought-after speaker. She founded the Rosa and Raymond Parks Institute in Detroit, which offers career training for 12-to-18-year-olds.

After suffering for a year with progressive dementia, Parks died in her apartment in Detroit on October 24, 2005. In her honor, the bus systems of Detroit and Montgomery placed black ribbons in the first four rows of their buses to reserve them for Rosa Parks until her funeral. Her memorial in Montgomery was heavily attended, and her remains were later moved to the U.S. Capitol rotunda, where she lay in state on October 31, making her the first woman and only the second African-American to receive this honor. Parks was buried alongside her husband and mother in Detroit's Woodlawn Cemetery. Per her instructions, her headstone reads only Rosa L. Parks, wife, 1913-2005.

The Legacy of the Woman

Many historians have said that if Rosa Parks had not challenged the gross unfairness of the Montgomery bus system, somebody else would have. In fact, the comedy movie *Barbershop* contains a riff by comedian Cedric the Entertainer saying that all she did was sit down. However, most white and African-American leaders believed that she displayed unusual courage. Just as importantly, she leveraged her prestige in the civil rights movement to do other good works, such as creating her institute.

Parks was also very wary about how her name was used and was not pleased when she believed somebody was exploiting it. The most famous example of this was when she sued LaFace Records and hip-hop artists OutKast for a song called *Rosa Parks*, which used her name without her permission. The lawsuit dragged on for years and many friends of Parks believed that her lawyers were using it for their own advantage. The suit was finally settled in April 2005, with an undisclosed sum of money being given by the defendants to Parks' institute.

Despite her celebrity status, Parks received most of her honors during the last part of her life. She received the NAACP's Spingarn Medal and the Martin Luther King Jr. Award. She was given the Presidential Medal of Freedom from President Bill Clinton in 1996 and, in 2000, Troy University in Montgomery created the Rosa Parks Library and Museum located on the corner where she boarded the bus for that fateful ride.

The Resources

Rosa Parks' life was made into a television movie, *The Rosa Parks Story,* starring Angela Bassett, in 2002, available on DVD. Parks also wrote *Rosa Parks: A Memoir*, designed for younger readers to learn about her life and the civil rights movement.

Other worthwhile books about Parks include *Rosa Parks*, Thomas Y. Crowell, 1973; *Quiet Strength*, Zondervan, 2000; *Rosa Parks*, Penguin Neo-classics, 2005; *She Would Not Be Moved*, New Press, 2005; *Rosa,* Henry Holt and Co., 2005; and *The Bus Ride That Changed History: The Story of Rosa Parks,* Houghton Mifflin, 2003.

34

Luciano Pavarotti,
Opera Singer

Who He Is

Who has not been entranced by the majesty and strength of Pavarotti's voice and presence? Few of our heroes exist in exalted and rarified worlds like opera. But this hero is one who transcends that world and makes himself and his art accessible to everyone.

He is a great popularizer but has not traded down. He is approachable without losing his majesty. And he is a singer of such control and majesty that even the uninitiated feel compelled to stop, look and listen when he sings, and they find themselves appreciating his extraordinary talent.

What Made the Man

Pavarotti was born on October 12, 1935, on the outskirts of Modena in north-central Italy. Pavarotti always portrayed his childhood as being idyllic, but the family was impoverished and crowded four members into a two-room apartment. Pavarotti's father had a fine tenor voice but decided not to pursue performing because of terminal stage fright. Instead, he supported the family as a baker. Pavarotti's mother helped financially by working in a cigar factory–hardly the heady stuff of the operatic world.

World War II would force the family from their home and make them displaced persons, living in a single room they rented from a farmer in the nearby countryside. It is here that the young Pavarotti developed an interest in farming. As he finished his schooling, he also developed an interest in sports in general, and soccer in particular.

After graduating from the Schola Magistrale, Pavarotti considered a career as a professional soccer player, but his mother argued him out of what she deemed a chancy career and encouraged the young Pavarotti to be a teacher. Pavarotti taught elementary school for 2 years, but his growing interest in music and recognition of his natural talents made him want to try to be an opera singer. He finally convinced his father to support his decision. The man agreed to give his son free room and board until Pavarotti was 30. After that, he would have to make a living on his own as best he could.

Pavarotti was all of 19 when he began studying music in earnest with Arrigo Pola. Pola, a respected music teacher and tenor living in Modena, knew that the family had little money to spare for music lessons, but was so impressed with the young tenor-to-be that he offered to teach Pavarotti for free. Pavarotti soon discovered, to his delight, that he had perfect pitch. This encouraged him to continue his training.

At about the same time Pavarotti was beginning his musical training, he met Adua Veroni, whom he married in 1961. Pavarotti's first teacher, Pola, moved to Japan in 1963, and Pavarotti began studies with Ettore Campogaliani, who had taught Pavarotti's childhood friend Mirella Freni (who was quickly building a reputation as a talented soprano).

Pavarotti supported his new family and his studies through a series of odd jobs, including returning to teaching and, of all things, selling insurance.

Pavarotti's early years of study only resulted in performing at a few recitals (without pay); frankly, he did not overly impress anyone. A nodule developed on his vocal cords, and he decided to give up singing. He later said that this decision freed him psychologically from the pressures to succeed. Fortunately, the nodule disappeared. He believed that this was a crucial element in finding his natural voice and creating the type of sound he had been struggling to achieve.

For whatever reason, Pavarotti post-nodule was a better singer, and he began to receive some recognition. He won the Achille Peri Competition, appearing as Rodolfo in a production of *La Boheme*. Pavarotti's appearance helped him secure his first agent, Alesandro Ziliani. With his help, Pavarotti appeared in *La Boheme* in Lucca and later as the Duke of Mantua in *Rigoletto*.

Pavarotti made his debut at Covent Garden in *La Boheme* in late 1963. The singer originally set to sing Rodolfo had a reputation for canceling at the last minute and the concert promoters wanted a singer they could rely on as a backup. Pavarotti agreed to learn the role without any guarantee that he would perform it, but got his chance when the original tenor, as expected, canceled after only one and one-half performances. Pavarotti received great recognition and began to make an impact in the opera community.

Things started happening fast for the young tenor after that. He made his debut at La Scala in 1965, again as Rodolfo, and made his American debut the same year in Miami as Edgardo in *Lucia di Lammermoor*. He had to cancel his 1968 debut at the New York Metropolitan Opera because of ill health. However, he made a successful tour of Australia, performed again at La Scala and Covent Garden, and recordings of his performances were starting to gain in popularity.

Pavarotti finally made a triumphant New York debut in 1972 in a production of *L'Elisir d'Amore* with the famous Joan Sutherland. This was followed by frequent television performances, including the first *Live From the Met* broadcast in 1977. His recordings began winning Grammy awards as well as platinum and gold discs.

In the 1980s Pavarotti's name became synonymous with opera. He set up the Pavarotti International Voice Competition for younger singers and performed with the winner. He was expanding his repertoire by releasing albums of popular standards. He performed in such huge venues as Hyde Park in London and the Great Hall of the People in Beijing, China.

In 1990, Pavarotti recorded the Puccini aria *Nessun Dorma* as the theme song of the World Cup in Italy. The song would go on to be Pavarotti's trademark song. The same year, he also made his first appearance as part of the Three Tenors (along with Placido Domingo and Jose Carreras) at the Baths of Caracalla in Rome with music director Zubin Mehta. The recording of the concert became the best-selling classical record of all time. Just for fun, he sang with Vanessa Williams in a 1998 *Saturday Night Live* (the only opera singer to ever appear on the show) and with Bono and the band U2 on their 1995 song *Miss Sarajevo*.

The early years of the 21st century saw Pavarotti going through some difficult times, including the breakup of his relationship with his long-term manager Herbert Breslin, the ending of his first marriage and his second marriage to his assistant Nicoletta Mantovani.

Health problems started to beset Pavarotti and limited his ability to perform. At age 69, he announced his farewell tour in 2004. He had to struggle with tax disputes in Italy. He underwent neck and back surgery and was diagnosed with pancreatic cancer in July 2006. After emergency surgery, Pavarotti began to recuperate and is hoping to resume the farewell tour in 2007.

The Legacy of the Man

Luciano Pavarotti will certainly go down in history as one of the most accomplished and popular tenors in classical music. He made the *Guinness Book of World Records* for receiving the most curtain calls (165) following a performance and for the Three Tenors best-selling classical album of all time.

However, Pavarotti was not a perfect performer. Although he was universally praised for his singing, his acting on stage was considered inferior and he struggled most of his early career to try to improve it. He also had to argue throughout his career that he could read music, but sometimes had difficulty following the orchestral parts.

Toward the end of his career, Pavarotti also gained a reputation for canceling performances, often at the last minute. This tendency led to his being banned in the late 1990s from ever performing with the Lyric Opera in Chicago, Illinois. And while his willingness to explore pop singing won him additional fans, many critics thought it was a waste of his time and talent. His 1980s attempt at romantic film comedy, *Yes, Giorgio*, was a critical and popular disaster.

However, most opera fans consider these mere distractions from the career of a truly special performer whose voice could take you into a different world.

The Resources

Many Pavarotti CDs are still available. His solo performances and appearances with the Three Tenors are on video. You can find more information about him at *www.lucianopavarotti.com.*

Books about Pavarotti include *Pavarotti: My Own Story*, Warner Books, 1982; *Luciano Pavarotti: The Myth of the Tenor*, Northeastern University Press, 1996; *The King and I: The Uncensored Tale of Luciano Pavarotti's Rise to Fame by His Manager, Friend and Sometime Adversary*, Doubleday, 2004; and *Pavarotti: Life With Luciano*, DIANE Publishing Company, 1998.

35

Eva Maria Duarte de Peron,
First Lady

Who She Is

Eva Peron was our hero because she always seemed larger than life–like Princess Di or Jacqueline Kennedy–and she managed somehow, remotely, to make us feel better about ourselves. She had a fascinating hold on the average person in Argentina and continues to exercise a fascination on the world.

Unfortunately, our heroine is not the stuff of greatness–rather an image of a beautiful, sophisticated, ambitious woman who knew how to manipulate the public.

What Made the Woman

Like many aspects of her life, the facts about Eva's birth are disputed. She was born Eva Maria Duarte on May 7, 1919, at what is believed by some to be the city of Junin in the province of Buenos Aires (other historians think she was born in the nearby village of Los Toldos). Eva, an illegitimate child, grew up with her mother and brothers at La Union farm. Eva arrived in Buenos Aires when she was 15, probably with the help of her mother.

She soon found herself facing the usual problems of any newcomer to a large and unfamiliar metropolis. She had no formal education and no connections in the city, and soon also discovered the rigid class system that ruled Buenos Aires' society. She eventually fell into work as a radio and film actress (many detractors claimed she got these jobs by sleeping her way to the top), and began making regular appearances in B-movies and radio soap operas. Some believe that she dyed her hair blonde during this time so she could look more like her favorite actress, Norma Shearer.

Just as Eva was making a name for herself, she met Colonel Juan Peron at a fundraiser to aid victims of the 1944 San Juan earthquake. The post-World War

II government of Argentina was then in constant turmoil. Thanks to his ability to relate to the common people (the descamisados) and his high-profile earthquake relief activities, Peron was considered a possible future president.

His political foes had Peron arrested because of his growing popularity. A widespread myth was that Eva supported Peron on her radio shows and organized a rally of thousands that helped free him from prison. In reality, Eva was still just an actress with no political clout, especially among the powerful labor unions. Her relationship with Peron continued to grow, even though she was not popular with Peron's colleagues.

Eva and Peron corresponded by letters and discussed the possibility of leaving Argentina upon Peron's release. They also had to face the fact that Peron might be killed in prison—not an irrational view, considering the political times.

Finally, a massive rally (actually organized by labor unions) resulted in Peron's release from prison on October 17, 1945. Shortly after his release, he married Eva. The newly freed Peron decided to turn his popularity into a serious bid for the nation's presidency, and he entered the 1946 elections.

Eva used her weekly radio show to extol Peron's virtues, and tried to show that her own upbringing (poor) somehow intimated his solidarity with the poor.

Eva went on the campaign trail with her husband (the first woman in Argentine politics ever to do so) and appeared at many events. These appearances were not popular with the upper classes, but the common people forged a strong bond with her. During the campaign, she encouraged the public to call her Evita (a rough Spanish equivalent to little Eva).

Peron was elected president of Argentina and Evita gradually acquired substantial power and influence in the new government. Her main job was to create a cult of personality around her husband and herself. However, the type of love she generated is believed to have actually hurt Peron's presidency. He was used to universal praise and was very sensitive to the slightest criticism—even managing to suggest that it could be viewed as an insult to the country, not just himself personally.

Evita stepped out upon the world stage when she started the heavily publicized Rainbow Tour of Europe in 1947. The tour was designed as a massive public relations effort to boost the image of the Peron government, which was increasingly seen as fascist. She was received well in the Spain of General Francisco Franco, but not as cordially in France and Italy. She called off a planned trip to the United Kingdom and returned home when she found out she would not be formally received by Queen Elizabeth II.

After returning to Argentina, Evita changed her style to simpler clothing and her hair pulled back into a bun. She was striving to be seen as a woman of her people. As part of this change of image, Evita began to focus on charity work. She created the Eva Peron Foundation to help build hospitals and orphanages (although some critics believed the foundation funds found their way back to the Perons).

In the general election of 1951, Evita decided to earn a place on the ballot as a vice-presidential candidate. Once she realized that even Juan Peron did not like this idea, Evita formally declined to run for vice president, and devoted her time to supporting her husband.

Part of this decision might also have been based on Evita's increasing physical incapacity. After Peron was re-elected, her health had deteriorated to the point where she could not stand without support from a wire frame worn under her dress. She was also using increasingly heavy doses of painkillers. Evita had developed uterine cancer that had spread and could not be completely removed. The end came quickly and Evita died on July 26, 1952, at the age of 33. The country entered an unprecedented period of national mourning.

Shortly after her death, plans were made to erect a monument in Evita's honor larger than the Statue of Liberty, with Evita's body on display to the public. However, Peron was overthrown in a military coup before the monument was completed and did not secure Evita's body when he fled. The new dictatorship removed the body from display and its whereabouts were unknown for years. From 1955 until 1971, all references to Juan Peron and Evita were forbidden. Finally, it was revealed that Evita's body had been interred in a crypt in Milan, Italy, under the name of Maria Maggi. The body was exhumed and sent to Spain, where Juan Peron, in exile, maintained the corpse in his home.

Juan Peron returned to Argentina and was again elected president in 1973. He died in office, and Isabel Peron, the vice president, became the first female head of state in the Americas. The body of Evita was briefly displayed next to Peron's, and she was finally laid to rest in the secure Duarte family tomb in La Recoleta Cemetery, Buenos Aires.

The Legacy of the Woman

Eva Peron was beloved by her people and almost universally despised by the ruling classes. Her name appeared almost everywhere during her brief reign; a city and even a star were named after her.

Despite a reputation for being ambitious, she was always careful to stress that everything she said or did in public was inspired by Peron. It is believed that she ultimately made herself subordinate to her husband's political agenda. However, she could be vindictive, and those who insulted or opposed her were often sent into exile.

Despite her shortcomings and reoccurring rumors of her and Peron's sympathy to Nazism and fascism, Evita remains a beloved figure to millions of Argentines and a popular subject for drama. The most famous version of her life (portraying her mostly as a villain) is the musical *Evita* by Andrew Lloyd Webber and Tim Rice. No matter her motivations, Eva Peron will be remembered as a popular cultural icon and as a pioneer in combining politics with show business.

The Resources

The sound tracks to the stage and movie versions of *Evita* are available on CD. The movie version, starring Madonna and Antonio Banderas, is available on DVD. Also available is the Argentine film, *Eva Peron: The True Story*. More information about her can be found at *www.evitaperon.org*.

Books on Evita include *Evita: The Real Life of Eva Peron*, W.W. Norton, 1996; *Evita: In My Own Words*, New Press, 2005; *Evita: An Intimate Portrait of Eva Peron*, Thames and Hudson, 1997; and *Eva Peron*, St. Martin's Press, 1997.

36

Elvis Aaron Presley, *Musician*

Who He Is

It would be difficult to imagine a more complicated hero than Elvis Presley. Here was a man of humble origins who revolutionized music and the contemporary culture with hip music, good looks, a sexy smile and a swagger. His every movement (many seen on television, including the famous *Ed Sullivan Show*) was followed by millions. His popularity–personal and musical–was unprecedented. So much so that even now, long after his death, his career, his estate at Graceland and his music continue to attract fans–fans who never saw him perform and are not even close to being his contemporaries.

Why is this man, truly a legend in his own time and beyond, a hero? He did not lead a nation or write great books or advance learning in any significant way. He was a farm boy with a limited education and seemingly little chance of success.

So popular is Elvis that even the former prime minister of Japan, an avid fan, wanted to experience the Elvis legend! President Bush took him to Graceland as part of an official visit to the United States.

In later life, his personal behavior was at best strange, almost as strange as his death. He had turned into an aging rocker with bizarre personal habits, a tendency to gain huge amounts of weight and a serious addiction to drugs–yet all is forgiven and forgotten.

What Made the Man

Reportedly a very shy child, Presley was born in modest circumstances to working-class parents in East Tupelo, Mississippi. He was an only child (his twin brother was stillborn). The family experienced some very awkward times when Presley's father was convicted of check forgery and sentenced to 3 years in the state work farm.

When he was just 10 years old, Elvis showed his talent for singing when he won second prize in a local contest. A year later, he bought his first guitar and took it with him wherever he went. His pastor gave him basic guitar lessons and set him on his way.

Once his father returned, the family settled a bit, but eventually moved to Memphis. It was in Memphis that the rather shy boy began to explore some of the African-American neighborhoods. He was later to be influenced by the music he heard there, and he met B.B. King and other blues musicians from the area.

During and after high school, he worked a variety of jobs–from driving a truck to laboring in a machine shop. But that would not be for long–he still had his music and was doing everything possible to absorb the style and tone of the southern blues.

His big break came when he met Sam Phillips of Sun Records. At that time–or so the story goes–Phillips was looking for a white man who could sing the black blues and boogie-woogie music–which Phillips was convinced would be a huge hit for a larger, white audience. In fact, most of Elvis' early efforts were really takeoffs of traditional country and western music, not the rock and roll influenced by the blues musicians that Elvis liked so much. So, naturally, he got a turn at the Grand Ole Opry and appearances on the live country music show *The Louisiana Hayride*.

By 1955, it was time to move up to the big time, and Elvis signed with Colonel Tom Parker, who proceeded to buy out the singer's contract with Sun Records and find him a home with the much larger RCA Victor. While Elvis was certainly talented, most historians and those knowledgeable about Elvis would say that it was the relationship with Parker that really moved his career. The Colonel was a masterful promoter and wasted no time in getting Elvis seen and heard.

In this process, television–just entering its golden age–was vital. As a medium, it had captivated the United States and replaced radio as the entertainment choice. Many famous entertainers were on television–often in variety shows that the whole family could enjoy. Among the notables were Milton Berle, Ed Sullivan, Steve Allen and the Dorsey Brothers. This was big-time entertainment and Parker used these promotions to make Elvis famous. And he soon became famous, especially with his controversial swinging hips, which scandalized and delighted middle America.

However, Colonel Tom was not through. The real money, according to Parker, was in movies. He signed Elvis with MGM studios, with Parker receiving a huge portion of the deal–as much as 50 percent. Nevertheless, Presley made a great deal of money from movies such as *Jailhouse Rock* and *Love Me Tender*–enormous box office hits. The movie business changed Presley's image from a risk-taking (even risqué) singer to a more sedate, wholesome entertainment figure.

Could Elvis ever lose popularity with his fans? A 2 year stint in the Army and a series of very mediocre movies did just that, helped along by the British invasion. Elvis seemed to be out of step, and he certainly had lost the exciting, cutting edge that had made him so popular and so threatening to adults. Now, through the 1960s, we get the watered down but very rich Elvis for whom music and movies were increasingly uninteresting.

However, 1968 would change all of that. This was his comeback year, thanks to very popular television specials and concerts in Las Vegas and other cities. The live Elvis, singing again, demonstrated once and for all that the King still had it. His tours over the next few years would be sold out city after city, including one done in Hawaii that was broadcast all over the world to an enormous audience!

But the return to popularity would not be smooth. By the time of his death in 1977, Elvis had taken on a peculiar persona–overweight, clothed in white jumpsuits and other odd costumes, using heavy makeup and, of course, taking a good deal of prescription drugs. There are countless stories of his odd behavior and even odder eating habits. The hard-edged rock and roller had turned into something very different in middle age (contrast Elvis, for example, with the Rolling Stones, who have never changed what they do).

The Legacy of the Man

Elvis' death exposed the great singer to a good deal of gossip, speculations and outright nastiness. It is very clear that this hero had come down a peg or two. His personal life seems to have been in shambles. At one point, it was suggested that he died of a heart attack, but in reality there were sufficient drugs of different kinds in his system to suggest either an accidental overdose or even suicide. Theories abound.

His personal relationships with various women throughout his life caused considerable scandal–especially his tendency to date very young women. There are those who believe that Elvis was gay, or at least bisexual, supported by long-term relationships with people he had known throughout his career, and his changing and erratic behavior later in life.

There can be no doubt that the artist and singer known as Elvis Presley brought to life a new kind of music that shocked, thrilled and dismayed audiences worldwide.

But there is no denying that he has become a cult figure to generations who never saw him or heard his music live. A whole industry has grown up around Elvis and Graceland, a very strange mixture of imitation and idolatry. However, if we set aside some very odd aspects of his life and culthood, there is still a great deal of music to enjoy and celebrate.

The Resources

Of course Elvis has a Website, even in death. Visit *www.elvis.com* for a variety of experiences. Naturally, you can also shop Elvis at *www.shopelvis.com*.

An excellent Website, the Rock and Roll Hall of Fame and Museum, is worth a visit for Elvis material and for a lot more as well. Visit *www.rockhall.com*.

37

Ronald Wilson Reagan, *President*

Who He Is

There was something irrepressible about Ronald Reagan—a smiling, warm and open individual who seemed greater than life. Perhaps he really was the consummate actor and the great communicator. In person, on television, on the radio—and, of course, in all his old movies—he exuded charm and charisma. His supporters were wild in their enthusiasm, just as his detractors found him too smooth, too refined and too rehearsed.

Perhaps not a very complicated man (he could never be accused of overmanaging his cabinet and advisers), he came from a small college (Eureka) and an even smaller town (Tampico) in Illinois. An athlete, sports announcer, Screen Actors Guild president, Democrat turned conservative Republican, he arrived on the political stage at a time when conservatism seemed out of favor with the voters. He redefined that political perspective—so fully, in fact, that he was able to use it as a springboard to national prominence and the presidency.

If nothing else, he was an enthusiastic and optimistic man who came to the nation's attention at a time of tense political and economic problems—high unemployment, inflation and waning international respect for American foreign policy.

What Made the Man

Born on February 6, 1911, the second son of Irish and English immigrants, he lived most of his life in Dixon, Illinois. Before settling in Dixon, the family moved a number of times, including a stint on the South Side of Chicago and Galesburg, Illinois. However, it was Dixon's small-town life that formed the man: student body president in high school, a gifted athlete in basketball, football and track, and a prominent member of the drama club. For 7 years, he worked as a life guard and was credited with saving 77 lives!

The real personality of the future actor, governor and president emerged when he began his collegiate studies at Eureka College. Again, he was elected student body president, and participated in drama, swimming and football. Reagan the activist first came to light at Eureka where he helped organize a student strike.

After graduation, he began his real political life, stumping for Franklin Delano Roosevelt (he was later a staunch defender of Harry Truman). This was a very unexpected political beginning for Mr. Republican.

By 1933, he made a name for himself as the local Des Moines, Iowa, radio announcer for the Chicago Cubs baseball team. His job was to announce Cubs home games–a very tricky task when you are sitting in a radio booth hundreds of miles away from the action! A testament to his cleverness is that using just a simple ticker tape feed, he was able to create a colorful and detailed game for the listeners. He used his vast imagination to fill in the rest–reportedly, he continued his play-by-play description of the game even when the ticker tape went off. He improvised by having the batter hitting a series of foul balls until the ticker tape came back on.

Most biographers, even good friends, would agree that his acting career in Hollywood at Warner Brothers was the stuff of B movies. During his Hollywood days, he first married (and later divorced) Jane Wyman, was active in the Screen Actors Guild, was called to active duty during World War II, and involved himself in local and national politics–particularly interesting was his support, as a Democrat, of Nixon, Eisenhower and other Republicans.

As important as any movie or television role was his marriage to Nancy Davis, the future and sometimes infamous Mrs. Ronald Reagan. By 1962, he had officially changed parties and was now a registered Republican. Many political pundits credit his famous television speech in support of the ultraconservative presidential candidate Barry Goldwater as the true beginning of his political career. The speech brought him into both the local and national limelight. In 1966, his popularity was so strong that he trounced Governor Pat Brown, a Democrat, in the California election.

The Legacy of the Man

The new governor wasted no time in starting to build his political empire, both within California and nationally. He practiced the famous guideline, "do not speak ill of other Republicans" and was generous to a fault in his support of not only conservatives but even moderate Republicans. (In fact, he burned few bridges: Witness the now famous wooing of conservative Democrats, the so-called Reagan Democrats of later years.)

By the time he was nominated in Detroit in July of 1980, there were few who did not believe that he would trounce the incumbent, Jimmy Carter. In fairness, Reagan's victory owed something to Carter's problems, his public perception, the state of the economy and the Iranian hostage crisis. But the fact remained: Reagan never varied his political agenda and hammered away at it until the American public saw his views as new, refreshing and optimistic. (As every student of history knows, it is one thing to win the presidency; it is another to govern effectively and to show real results.)

His critics saw his views of the world as simplistic–virulently anti-communist, for example; he used his famous evil empire concept throughout his presidency. There are many who will credit the fall of the Soviet Union to Reagan's huge increases in military spending, the so-called Star Wars initiative and constant pressure on the Soviet Union and its leaders (including the speech in Berlin when he challenged Mr. Gorbachev to tear down the wall).

And there are those who say that the fall of communism was inevitable. First of all, the Soviet Union was a financial wreck. Industries and employee productivity were non existent. The goods were shabby and the services even shabbier. Hard currency was non-existent and innovation for hard work or initiative was not rewarded. In addition, the Reagan administration supported an exhausting war in Afghanistan, which broke Soviet morale at home and depleted precious resources. Finally, new technologies (for the time) like fax machines allowed dissidents and others to smuggle information into the Soviet Union.

The Reagan team was perhaps most famous for its theory of economics, frequently called Reaganomics, or supply-side economics. The essentials of these policies were based on huge tax cuts (which many said benefited the rich), a massive, full-scale assault on inflation, deregulation of business, reduction in interest rates, increased military spending and increased deficits in the national debt (some of the same policies used by John F. Kennedy years before)! Whether critics liked Reagan's economic policies or not, the fact is that they worked. After a short recession, the economy grew at a rate that had not been seen for 25 years.

An important part of his national and economic view was the role of government– or rather, the limited role of government in Americans' lives. Reagan did everything humanely possible to bring about a reduction of government control and influence. He felt that government was the single, largest problem facing the United States at the time.

Despite scandals that would have brought down other administrations—he became known as the Teflon President—his popularity remained strong throughout his administration and he continued to be revered. His influence was so strong that for the first time in many years the Republicans controlled the Senate. His coalition of conservatives, Republicans and Democrats, helped fellow Republican George H.W. Bush succeed him as president.

By the time of his death at age 93, Ronald Wilson Reagan was thought of as one of the most successful and popular presidents since Franklin Roosevelt (oddly, they are often compared to each other, despite their political and government propensities). Personally energetic, loyal to a fault, charming, optimistic and consistent in his conservative message, he and his legacy endure as a great moment in American history.

The Resources

An entire history of Reagan's presidency, among many other items, can be found if you visit *www.reaganfoundation.org*.

For an insider's view (and a very favorable one) of Ronald Reagan, read *Ronald Reagan: The Power of Conviction and the Success of His Presidency*, Westview Press, 2004. The book is available at *www.barnesandnoble.com* as well as *www.amazon.com*.

38

Syngman Rhee, *President*

Who He Is

Syngman Rhee was a very complicated man and his personal and political life is equally controversial. First and foremost, he was a nation builder and, like many before him, his methods were not always the best. On the other hand, he had a vision and a determination to free Koreans from Japanese dominance and to build a nation-state. Are the means justified by the ends? Many would say not.

Unfortunately, nation building is a complicated process that has to accommodate many views and many plans. Not everyone will agree about the best methods–witness the current conflict in Iraq or review American history in detail to see the conflicts, indecision and slow progress that building a nation can involve. Further, personal ambition and the cult of personality can often obscure the larger, national goal. This certainly reflects the role of Rhee in building a Korean state.

> As a hero, Syngman Rhee was certainly flawed. Yet he had tremendous support, including that of the United States, which may have used him for its anti-communist political agenda at the time. Nevertheless, it is safe to say that millions of Koreans loved and respected him for making a modern Korea a political reality.

What Made the Man

Syngman Rhee was born in the Wanghai Province of Korea on April 26, 1875. His family had strong ties to one of Korea's dynastic rulers. He attended an American Methodist mission school, Paejae High School, after completing the more traditional Korean Confucian education.

Rhee became interested in the nationalist cause in Korea, and he joined the reformist Independence Club in 1897. He was imprisoned and tortured for his activities in this club. While in prison, he wrote a political testament, *The Spirit of Independence,* which was widely circulated in the United States. He also converted to Christianity at this time.

After Rhee's release from prison in 1904, he traveled to the United States, where he attended university and eventually obtained a Ph.D. from Princeton. He stayed in the United States for a total of 6 years and returned to Korea in 1911 as a YMCA teacher-evangelist. Korea was now under the brutal control of the Imperial Japanese, and Rhee was an outspoken critic of the occupation. Sensing that he was close to being arrested again, he left Korea in 1912. This time he traveled to Hawaii, where he would remain until 1940. Rhee continued his work to achieve Korean independence, but his efforts were often blocked by Korean political and church leaders.

Before leaving Korea for the first time, Rhee went through a traditionally arranged marriage, but his wife died in 1933 after giving birth to one son. Rhee met his second wife, Francesca Donner, a native Austrian, when he traveled to the League of Nations in Geneva, Switzerland, in 1933, to present the case for an independent Korea. They would remain married for the rest of their lives and later adopt a son. Francesca would become Korea's first lady.

At that time, Korean politics under Japanese rule were chaotic. A provisional Korean government had been established in Shanghai, China, after a failed uprising against the Japanese in 1919. Rhee was named president of the Korean Provisional Government in Exile. As before, his strong views and ego led to strained relations with the others in the provisional government, and he was impeached in absentia and replaced with President Kim Koo. Rhee refused to recognize the impeachment and still insisted that he was the president of an independent Korea.

After Korea was liberated from the Japanese in 1945, Rhee returned to his native country. He was encouraged to do so by a base of American conservatives and the American military occupation authorities. He was elected president of Korea in 1948 by a vote in parliament and formally took over power from the U.S. military. He soon attempted to put through efforts to start a national coalition that would unite most of Korea's battling political partisans. Partly because of the national mood of the country and Rhee's tendency not to compromise, these efforts failed.

Soon after his election to the presidency, Rhee campaigned hard for a separate South Korea. He was staunchly anti-communist and could not stomach the idea of negotiating with the Soviet-controlled leaders of the North. Rhee's government quickly took on an authoritarian role, with his national security forces free to arrest and torture anyone they suspected of being a Communist or a North Korean agent. His government is also believed to have instigated several massacres in response to what Rhee saw as uprisings by leftists.

Rhee's worst fears were confirmed when a North Korean offensive in 1950 effectively started the Korean War. The war was not a shining example of Rhee's presidential abilities. He encouraged panicking South Koreans to stay in Seoul while he and his family took refuge away from the city. He blew up bridges over the Han River that trapped many South Koreans in areas that would soon fall to the North Korean army.

Once the war became a stalemate after a United Nations offensive and counterattack by North Koreans and Chinese, Rhee delayed a cease-fire by constantly refusing to accept repeated proposals. Rhee's ultimate goal was to use the war to destroy the North Korean government and unite the two countries as one, with himself as president. When he was guaranteed massive economic and military support from the United States, he finally agreed to a cease-fire, to the establishment of a demilitarized zone (DMZ) between the two countries and to maintain a separate North Korea and South Korea.

Rhee was re-elected president in 1952 and 1956. During portions of the war he had been able to create the equivalent of today's exclusive economic zones by claiming sovereignty over the waters around the Korean peninsula. Rhee continued to try to consolidate his power and pushed amendments through the parliament that would have allowed direct election of the president. To enhance his position, he even declared martial law as a means of persuasion.

Finally, in 1960, amid accusations of a rigged election, and in real danger of being lynched, Rhee fled South Korea with help from the CIA. After his departure, his successor revealed that Rhee had misappropriated at least $20 million from the government. Until his death from a stroke in 1965, Rhee and his family lived in exile in Hawaii. After his death, his body was returned to South Korea and he was interred in the South Korean National Cemetery.

The Legacy of the Man

The legacy of Syngman Rhee is complicated and often disputed by historians and political scientists. Few doubt that Rhee was committed to an independent and democratic Korea, and was willing to put himself at risk (including prison and torture) to help achieve this goal.

At the same time, he seemed to mistrust the very process he advocated, and, once he became president, used his powers to crush any dissent and establish an almost fascist-like authoritarian regime. It can also be argued that his tactics during the Korean War led to the unnecessary deaths of thousands of South Koreans and United Nations soldiers by prolonging the conflict—in theory, long past the point when it could have been resolved.

In general, how the Koreans feel about the legacy of Rhee depends on their political views. Conservatives tend to see him as a dedicated anti-communist and national patriarch. Liberals view him more as a ruthless autocrat who stole from his own country. It is interesting to note that in Korea Rhee is never formally referred to as president but as baksa, which means doctor. In contrast, Kim Koo, his long-time political rival, is referred to as seonsaeng, which means teacher and is considered a higher honorific.

Whether viewed as tyrant or political visionary, Rhee clearly wanted the best for his country and helped shepherd it through some of its most difficult times.

The Resources

Much information can be found on Syngman Rhee by visiting *www.asiasource. com*. Note that this Website is not devoted exclusively to Rhee, but includes other Asian leaders.

Other material on Rhee includes *Korea Flaming High: Excerpts From Statements by President Syngman Rhee During the Crucial Year of 1953*, Office of Public Information, Republic of Korea, 1954 ; *Syngman Rhee: The Man Behind the Myth*, Dodd-Mead, 1954; *Fall of Syngman Rhee*, University of California Institute of the East, 1983; and *Syngman Rhee Through Western Eyes*, Office of Public Information, Republic of Korea, 1954.

39

Jackie Robinson, *Athlete*

Who He Is

Many of us would think ill of a world so segregated that there were actually two major league baseball organizations—one for whites and the other for blacks. However, it was not just baseball that was out of bounds for promising African-Americans—it was most of contemporary life, including the majority of other sports, business, education and employment.

Finding yourself the only black athlete in the major leagues is hard to imagine. What must it be like to be shunned by fellow athletes and fans alike? Imagine traveling across the United States and being forced to take different accommodations from the rest of your teammates? Try to think of the courage it took to stand up against such social customs. Not only did Jackie Robinson need to break the color barrier, he had to do it as a better, faster and stronger player than the rest of his teammates—and the rest of the National League.

What Made the Man

Jack Roosevelt Robinson was born on January 31, 1919, in Cairo, Georgia. His mother, Mallie, moved the family to Pasadena, California. Robinson and his four older siblings grew up in a working-class neighborhood where racial prejudice was common. As a child, he was most comfortable playing sports and tried his hand at just about anything: baseball, basketball, dodgeball, football, golf, marbles, soccer and tennis.

Starting in 1939, Robinson attended the University of California, Los Angeles (UCLA) after excelling in sports at Pasadena Junior College. He continued his athletic success at UCLA, where he was a star player on the football, basketball, track and baseball teams. Robinson was the first athlete in the university's history to letter in four different sports.

Robinson's glory days at UCLA, sometimes tainted by the ever-present sting of racism, did not carry him all the way to graduation. He left school his junior year in 1941 due to financial difficulties, and enlisted in the U.S. Army during World War II. His battalion, the U.S. 761st Tank Battalion, was a segregated one, and although he was at first refused admission to Officer Candidate School, the strong-willed Robinson was finally accepted, graduating as a first lieutenant. One day, while he was training at Fort Hood, Texas, he—like Rosa Parks some years later—refused to sit in the back of a public bus. Robinson was court-martialed for insubordination, never making it to Europe with his unit. All charges were eventually dismissed and he received an honorable discharge from the Army in 1944.

In 1944, Robinson played shortstop for the Kansas City Monarchs in the Negro American League. He caught the attention of a scout who worked for Branch Rickey, the Brooklyn Dodgers' president and general manager. Rickey soon decided that Robinson had the strength, courage and, of course, skills to become the first African-American professional baseball player. In 1946, Robinson was assigned to play for the Montreal Royals, the top minor league affiliate of the Dodgers. He played second baseman and led the International League with a .349 batting average, while also stealing 40 bases and carrying the team to the Little World Series championship. The team as well as the fans in Montreal respected and welcomed Robinson almost overwhelmingly during his stay in their city. But that kind of support would soon come to an end for him—for a while, anyway.

In February of 1946, Robinson married his college sweetheart and girlfriend of 5 years, Rachel Islum. The couple had two sons and one daughter and led a full family life. On April 15, 1947, at Ebbets Field in Brooklyn, Robinson made his major league debut as the Dodgers' first baseman. He was harassed by players and fans throughout that entire first season, having to put up with, for example, pitchers throwing at his head, base runners attempting to injure him with their sharp cleats and black cats being thrown onto the field. He took verbal abuse not only from players on other teams but also from his very own teammates. The St. Louis Cardinals threatened to go on strike against Robinson's presence on the field.

An aggressive man by nature, one of the motivating factors behind Robinson's unusually quiet strength was the understanding between him and Rickey that he was chosen to integrate baseball in part because he had promised to be able to practice self-control even when times got hard. Robinson let his game performances do the work. By the end of his first season, he had achieved a batting average of .297 in 151 games, and led the league with 29 stolen bases. He was named the league's Rookie of the Year, a sign that he was definitely gaining the respect of fans and other players. In fact, other major league teams soon followed the Dodgers' lead and started hiring African-American players.

In 1949, Robinson was named the National League's Most Valuable Player after completing a fantastic season. He led the league both in hitting with .342 and steals with 37, all while batting in a career high of 124 runs. Although he played his rookie season with the Dodgers as a first baseman, he spent most of his career at second base. Throughout his 10 seasons with Brooklyn, Robinson saw the team win six National League pennants as well as the World Series in 1955 against their long-time rival, the New York Yankees. Robinson played in the last game of his professional career on September 30, 1956. He finished his career with a batting average of .311, 137 home runs, 734 runs batted in and 19 steals home.

After his retirement, Robinson ventured into the business world. From 1956 to 1964, he was the vice president of Chock Full O' Nuts, which is still a beloved café and coffee company in New York City. He also co-founded Freedom National Bank of Harlem and a construction company that focused on helping black Americans become homeowners.

In 1997, 50 years after Robinson's first season with the Dodgers, Major League Baseball (MLB) permanently retired his uniform, No. 42, from all of its teams. And in 2004, it named April 15 Jackie Robinson Day, to be celebrated each year in every league ballpark.

The Legacy of the Man

Robinson helped with the civil rights movement in any way that he could. He met Dr. Martin Luther King Jr. on more than one occasion and lent his time, money and presence to the cause of racial justice. He was a board member of the National Association for the Advancement of Colored People (NAACP) and was also on the board of advisers for the Harlem YMCA. In 1956, Robinson was awarded the Spingarn Medal, which is given yearly by the NAACP to an African-American who performs acts of distinguished merit and achievement.

Robinson appeared as himself in the 1950 movie *The Jackie Robinson Story*, and wrote an autobiography called *I Never Had It Made: An Autobiography of Jackie Robinson*, which was published in 1972.

Jackie Robinson literally changed the face of baseball when he became the first African-American to play in the major leagues. Although he was up against harsh, racist treatment, he remained strong through it all and came out on top as a true champion. His team won six pennants during the 10 seasons that he played with them, and he was inducted into the National Baseball Hall of Fame in 1962. Because of his heroic efforts, generations of African-American and other minority athletes have taken, and will continue to take, their rightful places as equals in the professional world of sports.

Shortly before his death in 1972, he was asked to throw out the first pitch at that year's World Series. That same year, Rachel started the Jackie Robinson Development Corporation, which builds low- and moderate-income housing. In 1973, she founded the Jackie Robinson Foundation, a not-for-profit national organization that helps deserving underprivileged minority youths by providing them with 4 year scholarships. In October of 2002, Robinson was posthumously awarded the Congressional Gold Medal, which Rachel accepted in a ceremony in the Capitol rotunda. Robinson, who also received the Presidential Medal of Freedom from Ronald Reagan in 1984, is only the second baseball player to receive the Congressional Gold Medal.

Jackie Robinson's legend continues through his family as well as through his memorable performances on the field of baseball and in the field of life.

The Resources

To delve further into the life of Jackie Robinson, read his wife's book, *Jackie Robinson: An Intimate Portrait*, Abradale/Abrams, 1998.

The Rolling Stones,
Musicians

Who They Are

If there are entertainment heroes with more lives than a cat, this is the group. Year after year, no matter how old they get, they appear at major venues throughout the world and entertain their ever-aging audiences with some of the greatest songs from the 1960s and 1970s. Even though the band, creatively, belongs somewhat to the past, fans love them anyway. Perhaps they represent the nostalgia that everyone craves—our time was the best, after all.

Why are they are heroes, despite their bad-boy image, drugs and decadent life? Well, they are heroes probably because they are bad boys, wild and decadent—and very entertaining. If nothing else, fans love the high energy level of Jagger on stage, even though he is in his 60s!

What Made the Group

The Rolling Stones are one of the most famous and popular rock and roll bands in history, making music for over 40 years and still going strong. The band's consistent members are Mick Jagger, Keith Richards and Charlie Watts. Other members included, and in some cases still include, co-founder Brian Jones, Mick Taylor, Ron Wood, Bill Wyman and keyboardist Ian Stewart (who was also the group's tour manager).

A fateful meeting between British schoolmates Jagger and Richards with Brian Jones began what would be the Rolling Stones (Jones came up with the idea of using the title of a Muddy Waters song as the name of the band). The band recruited Ian Stewart on piano and Bill Wyman as the bassist. After a series of drummers, the band brought in jazz-influenced Charlie Watts, who would stay with the group throughout its history.

The group was originally more interested in rhythm and blues (R&B) music, rather than what was considered rock and roll music at the time. The Stones quickly made a name for themselves, appearing at the Marquee Club in London, and soon had their own permanent club, The Crawdaddy Club in Richmond.

They were considered one of the best live acts in London and even the Beatles stopped by to check them out.

Thanks to a tip by George Harrison, Decca Records signed the Stones to a recording contract. Their first single was a cover version of *Come On* by Chuck Berry. The band was establishing a following for R&B, a music form that was still largely unfamiliar to the broader American rock audience. Their anti-Beatles street-tough and dangerous look also made them a fan favorite.

Until the release of the seminal record, *Out of Our Heads*, in 1965, most of the Stones' recordings were cover versions of other songs. Their manager encouraged them to write their own material, and the new album finally saw the beginnings of the collaboration between Jagger and Richards. The U.S. version of the album would contain seven original Rolling Stones songs, including the rock and roll icon, *I Can't Get No Satisfaction*. This record firmly established the Rolling Stones as rock stars in the United States.

Unfortunately, this new success with original music changed the dynamics of the band, with Jagger and Richards being commonly perceived as the band's leaders. This did not sit well with original founder Brian Jones and he went through a period of increasing depression and drug abuse.

Drugs would also create a crisis for Jagger and Richards. The police raided a drug-infused party held at Richards' Sussex home on February 12, 1967, and confiscated some amphetamine diet pills from Jagger and the ashes from purported marijuana pipes. Jagger protested the pills were readily and legally available in Italy. English authorities found both Jagger and Richards guilty of possession of illegal drugs. Jagger was sentenced to 3 months in jail and a fine, Richards was sentenced to a year in jail. After public protest, the sentences were either quashed or reduced to probation.

The success of the band was leading to discord between Jagger and Richards in the late 1960s, but this period would see the Stones return to their R&B roots and record some of their most popular songs, including *Jumpin' Jack Flash*, *Street Fighting Man* and *Sympathy for the Devil*. The Rolling Stones were now being referred to as the world's greatest rock and roll band.

Life was not going so well for co-founder Brian Jones who was by now taking more and more drugs and acting erratically. His behavior led to him being forced out of the band in 1969. He took refuge in his Cotchford Farm house. A month after his arrival, he was found dead at the bottom of his swimming pool. The death was ruled a suicide, although there have been consistent rumors of foul play.

Some critics began dismissing the Stones as irrelevant by the late 1960s and were enamoured of the new guitar bands such as Cream, Free and Led Zeppelin. To offset this image of being over the hill, the band planned a major concert tour of the United States. The tour culminated in a free concert at the Altamount Music Festival near San Francisco. The concert promoters had hired members of the Hell's Angels motorcycle gang for security, and the intoxicated guards beat up several concertgoers and reportedly stabbed and killed one man.

Even with this tragic incident, the 1969 tour was a triumph and the Stones were playing some of their best music. As the group progressed into the 1970s, it began to fragment. Disagreements between Jagger and Richards increased. Mick Taylor left the band because he believed he was not being properly credited for his work. And Jagger became less interested in the music than in traveling in jet-set social circles. The little music they produced during this period reflected this drifting.

The band was in danger of completely falling apart and, although they remained fan favorites, critics in the 1970s were increasingly dismissing their new music. This changed with the release of *Some Girls*, widely considered the best Rolling Stones album. Richards was making a concerted effort to kick his drug habits. The band again started achieving critical and audience success with the release of albums like *Tattoo You*, but the relationship between Jagger and Richards remained tenuous at best. Ron Wood was developing his own drug problems and would be fired from the band, and Jagger was attempting to record as a solo artist (with mixed success).

The death of long-time band member Ian Stewart in 1985 started motivating the band to reconcile their differences and make music again. The group released more albums, such as *Bridges to Babylon*, *Steel Wheels* and *A Bigger Bang*, and started touring extensively in the 1990s and into the 21st century (without Bill Wyman, who had retired). The band continues to tour the world, much to the delight of millions of fans.

The Legacy of the Group

The Rolling Stones are still a vital rock band, creating new music and rocking the house. Even though they are entering their 60s, Jagger and company continue to put out some of the most energetic music of any rock band.

Whether they were really the world's greatest rock and roll band is certainly open to debate, but their output in the 1960s and 1970s contains some of the most influential and covered rock songs in history. They managed (for the most part) to survive the costs of fame and fortune, as well as a creatively dry period in the 1990s, to once again emerge as a rock band that still has something to prove.

Who can say how long they will continue to perform? The band has forged a strong bond with their older fans, while still attracting younger fans who enjoy the band's sound and bad-boy image. Perhaps they are such a long-lived band simply because they and their fans agree that they know it's only rock and roll, but they like it.

The Resources

All of the Rolling Stones music (including solo efforts by Jagger, Richards, Watts and Wyman) is available individually or in boxed sets on CD. The documentary *Gimme Shelter*, about the band's infamous Altamount concert, is available on video. Also, an unusual movie about a wasted rock star called *Performance*, starring Jagger and Anita Pallenberg, is available on VHS. Information on new music and concert dates, as well as band history, can be found on *www. rollingstones.com*.

Books about the band include *The True Adventures of the Rolling Stones*, Chicago Review Press, 2000; *The Rolling Stones: In the Beginning*, Firefly Books, 2006; and *According to the Rolling Stones*, Planeta, 2000.

41

Franklin Delano Roosevelt, *President*

Who He Is

Franklin Delano Roosevelt was an odd contradiction as a man and politician. The 32nd president of the United States was both one of the most popular presidents of all time and seemingly one of the most complex. Here was a man who had unlimited compassion for the common man but could be aloof and distant when it came to matters of refugees and the plight of millions of Jews entering concentration camps.

How do we understand this man? Was he the great political genius or, as some would suggest, simply the right man in the right place at the right time? How are we to really know a man who managed to keep his personal life secret from the nation–rumored extramarital affairs, his handicap from polio and even his off-again, on-again relationship with his own wife, Eleanor Roosevelt, a growing political luminary in her own right.

Despite all the questions, Franklin Roosevelt has survived the rigors of investigation and the ebb and flow of historical criticism not only to be hailed as a great hero but to be truly idolized for the next 50 years for his accomplishments–no matter how they were perceived.

What Made the Man

Born in January of 1882, Franklin was the only child of a wealthy Democratic New York family from which he gained all the privileges of life–including trips to Europe and the finest private education: the Groton School, Harvard and Columbia Law School. He learned German and French, and was highly influenced by both his mother, Sara, and his vibrant, crusading Republican uncle, Theodore Roosevelt, president of the United States.

Roosevelt married a distant cousin, Eleanor. They seemingly were an odd couple: He was popular, outgoing, charming and sociable while she was shy, introverted and did not like social occasions. Her early wish was to stay home and raise children. They ended up having six children, five of whom survived into adulthood.

What really complicated Roosevelt's early adult years was the affair that he had with his secretary, Lucy Mercer, and the very poor relationship between his wife and mother. After a time, the Roosevelts started living apart, although they remained married–seemingly as political allies and friends, rather than as husband and wife.

A measure of the man is the fact that when he contracted polio in 1921, he desperately resolved not to let the resulting paralysis affect his life, his career or the public's perception of his abilities and personal strengths. The Roosevelt era was one in which a public figure, like a president, could actually acquire sympathy and support from the media, and thus hide, or at least manage, his handicap in public.

In an effort to assist others suffering from the ravages of polio and paralysis, Roosevelt went on to found what is now known as the March of Dimes.

Roosevelt the politician first came to light in his victory in the New York State Senate, in what had been traditionally a safe Republican district. He worked for reform in New York, vigorously opposing the Democratic machine in New York, known as Tammany Hall, first organized by Boss Tweed and known for its remarkable ability to garner votes, corrupt government and generate millions of dollars from its various, creative enterprises.

His first taste of Washington came when he was appointed assistant secretary of the Navy in the Wilson administration. His first attempt at national office was in 1920 when he was nominated for vice president on the Democratic ticket, which was soundly defeated by the Republican Warren G. Harding. Politics over, he moved back to New York state to practice law and retire from public life–or so he said!

By 1928, the fire was back in him and he ran as a reform governor in New York–ironically with the help and support of Tammany Hall, his avowed enemy. This was just one of the many political compromises Roosevelt was to make over his long career. His tinkering with greater government involvement in social and economic affairs would begin in New York and would ultimately find greater and more expansive expression in Washington.

Campaigning during the Great Depression, Roosevelt was the candidate for less government, sound currency and tight fiscal responsibility–an amazing irony considering the New Deal that was to come. Roosevelt defeated Hoover, winning the 1932 election. Government would never be the same. Throughout his terms in office, he enjoyed large pluralities in the popular polls and had the strong backing of an increasingly Democratic Congress–making his plans and programs all that much easier.

The Legacy of the Man

The Roosevelt administration concentrated on finding ways to bring immediate relief to the general public–as much as 25 percent of the American work force had no employment or marginal employment at best. The banking system was in chaos, commodities prices were the lowest in years, farmers were forced off the land and industrial production by any measure had plummeted to new lows.

In response, program after program was introduced into Congress and almost immediately passed–seemingly without much examination. Government involvement in business and industry was on the march and seemingly nothing would stop it. However, one obstacle did show up, the Supreme Court, which ruled against the administration's efforts on a number of occasions. Controversy erupted with an effort by Roosevelt to pack the Supreme Court by raising its membership above nine–with, of course, judges who would support New Deal legislation.

At the same time, he was actively working to advance the cause of certain Democrats, especially less-conservative ones in the Deep South. Many, supporters among them, objected to such attempts to put so much power in the hands of a sitting president. Indeed, many historians consider this the greatest display of personal arrogance ever seen in government. Both activities would cast enormous shadows on Roosevelt and his personal reputation.

While it is fairly clear, with hindsight, that the various New Deal programs did not end the depression of the 1930s, it is also the case that war, or rather preparations for war, did end the depression. By 1941, approximately one million people were out of work–a fraction of the unemployment of 10 years earlier.

If Franklin Roosevelt is truly a hero, it is for his efforts and leadership before and during the Second World War. He clearly understood the importance of reversing 20 or more years of isolationism in light of the international threats of fascism. He saw an impending change in the balance of power in the world, one that would ultimately hurt the United States and its interests, domestically and internationally.

Some historians charge that Roosevelt was far too willing to get into a fight, that until the Japanese attack, the United States had no business being a part of the war. Lend Lease and other covert activities were clearly a signal to the world that the democracies would maintain at least some semblance of solidarity.

If Roosevelt's position during the war were ever to be justifiably challenged, it would be in reference to Russia. Many believe that he was too old and too sick to deal with Stalin and the Russians demands in Eastern Europe. Roosevelt was pre-occupied with Stalin's commitment to attack Japan once the European fighting was finished—a promise that many felt Stalin had absolutely no intention of keeping in any significant way.

So, how do we judge Roosevelt? He was president for longer than any other man, and had been on center stage through some of the most tumultuous times in modern American history. He was the eternal optimist, the leader, the wartime president, the grand statesman and a larger-than-life figure. He came from wealth, yet challenged traditional notions of the responsibilities and rights of the rich—increasing income and excise taxes to the highest in the nation's history.

The other Roosevelt was seen as arrogant, prejudiced (having done little in the arena of civil rights, for example), obsessed with control and power, a profligate with the public's wealth, and a believer in big government, bigger budget deficits and higher taxes. He shaped modern American government, its role in everyday life, like no other president. His legacy, like Social Security, continues—a little shaky at times, but still monumental.

The Resources

Franklin Delano Roosevelt's personal and presidential papers are at his library in Hyde Park, New York. Visit *www.fdrlibrary.marist.edu* for more details.

For more information specifically about the war years and his relationship with Winston Churchill, consider the book, *Franklin and Winston: An Intimate Portrait of an Epic Friendship,* Random House Trade Paperbacks, 2004. It is highly rated by readers on *www.amazon.com.*

42

Anwar Sadat,
President

Who He Is

For hundreds of years, Arab culture and Arab political power were in serious decline. The so-called Ottoman Empire was referred to as the sick man of Europe. The Europeans had managed to get de facto control over much of the Middle East and North Africa. But times were changing. Egyptians, through the efforts of Gamal Nasser and other patriots, took control of Egypt and the Suez Canal, the most important link between Asia and Europe.

In this environment, a junior to Nasser grew to political maturity. His name was Anwar Sadat. Resolutely pro-Arab and just as vehemently anti-Israel, this man grew in stature to become the leader of Egypt, responsible for solving the Jewish question.

Is Sadat our hero because he is an Arab nationalist? Is he our hero because he retained strong political and economic control of Egypt–without dissent? No–he is our hero because he adapted to and changed the political reality of his time– moving from a militant to a national hero, accepting the state of Israel in fact and earning world recognition as a recipient of the Nobel Peace Prize.

What Made the Man

Sadat was born December 25, 1918, in the village of Mit Abul Al-Kum, Al-Minufah, to an impoverished family. His father was Egyptian and his mother was Sudanese. He eventually graduated from the Royal Military Academy in Cairo in 1938 as a signal corps officer. Before the start of World War II, Sadat joined the Free Officers Movement, a group of military officers who worked to remove the British from control of Egypt.

While in the Royal Academy, Sadat met a man who would have a profound effect on his life and the entire country, Gamal Nasser. Many Egyptian army officers were sympathizers with the Nazi armies fighting in northern Africa, hoping their victory would be a catalyst for Egyptian independence. After the Axis powers invaded Libya and made a push into Egypt in 1941 to attempt to seize the Suez Canal, Sadat plotted with German spies to help expel the British (his actions included trying to send sensitive information to German General Erwin Rommel).

Sadat's efforts were discovered and he was imprisoned by the British. He escaped from prison in 1944 and, with the help of freedom sympathizers, successfully hid from the British through the war. He resurfaced into public life in 1945 and immediately resumed his actions against British rule.

Sadat participated in the successful assassination of Amin Osman, an English-sympathizing Egyptian politician, in 1946. Sadat's role was discovered, and he was imprisoned again. During this second stay in jail, Sadat taught himself French and English, but the hardships of imprisonment took their toll over the long run.

Sadat and other co-conspirators in the plot against Osman went on trial in 1948, but the trial took a backseat to the 1948 Arab-Israeli War. The war was the Arab response to the creation of an independent state of Israel from what had been Palestine. The war would be the first of several pitting Arabs against Israelis.

The Arabs were stunned by the Israeli victory in the 1948 war and many, such as Nasser and Sadat, blamed the corrupt leadership of Egypt with the military debacle. Sadat was eventually released and drifted for a while, getting involved in several unsuccessful business ventures, and even trying his hand at acting. Sadat had been married early in his life, and in 1949 divorced his first wife, Ehsan Madi, to marry Jihan Raouf, who was barely 16 at the time. They would have three daughters and one son.

This unsettled period would end when he re-established contact with Nasser. Nasser and his followers were heavily involved in plotting to overthrow the increasingly corrupt government of King Farouk and his cronies. Nasser led a series of riots in 1952 that destroyed foreign-owned businesses in Cairo and finally showed Egypt's playboy king for the incompetent ruler that he was. The public quickly lost patience with the government.

Nasser and his followers carried out a successful coup against the government in July 1952. Nasser summoned his old colleague Sadat back to Cairo from the Sinai. After a series of miscommunications, Sadat emerged as the member of the coup who broadcast the news to the public. Farouk fled the country and many members of his government were either exiled or imprisoned.

Sadat was now a part of the new Egyptian government of Nasser, but his early assignments were not impressive. He edited the new regime's newspaper, and served as secretary-general of the Islamic Congress and National Union, the forerunner of Egypt's only political party. The importance of Sadat's jobs grew and he was a major advocate of Egypt's involvement in the disastrous Yemen civil war.

Soon after, Nasser's government started the 1967 Six-Day War with Israel. Egypt suffered a staggering defeat by the Israelis, almost destroying Nasser's regime. Recognizing his time in office might be growing short, Nasser appointed Sadat vice president. Nasser died of a heart attack in 1970 and Sadat was quickly confirmed as his successor. He cemented his hold on power in the Corrective Revolution of 1971, and signed a treaty of friendship with the Soviet Union.

Sadat's first years as president were full of surprises. He extended a cease-fire with the Israelis on the Suez front and announced plans to reopen the canal. Because he could not secure Soviet military support for a showdown with Israel, he expelled all the Soviet advisers from Egypt, hoping to gain some assistance from the United States.

The United States did not pay enough attention for Sadat's liking, and, along with Syria, he attacked Israel in 1973. At first, Egyptian forces were more successful than before and crossed the Suez Canal. However, they were quickly repulsed by an Israeli counterattack and Sadat found himself in a precarious position until intervention by the United States and Soviet Union led to a cease-fire.

At this time, Sadat took a chance by aligning himself with the United States, hoping shuttle diplomacy would lead to a long-term peace agreement with Israel.

Sadat surprised the world by visiting Israel and addressing the Knesset in 1977. U.S. President Jimmy Carter stepped in personally to move along the peace talks by bringing Sadat and Israeli Prime Minister Menachem Begin together at Camp David. The diplomatic efforts led to two major agreements for permanent peace and Palestinian autonomy. The final agreements were signed in 1979. Other Arab countries saw the agreement as being detrimental to Arab interests and withdrew their ambassadors from Egypt.

By the late 1970s, Sadat's open-door economic policies and peace efforts with Israel caused disillusionment among many Egyptians. In 1981, he arrested hundreds of politicians and silenced the media in an effort to keep power.

However, it was too late. On October 6, 1981, as Sadat was reviewing a military parade, he was assassinated by Muslim radicals. The murder shocked the West, which sent prominent government figures to his funeral. In contrast, the Egyptian public reaction to Sadat's death was tepid and the president of the Sudan was the only Arab head of state to attend his funeral.

The Legacy of the Man

How Anwar Sadat is viewed varies wildly between the West and the Middle East. Most Westerners view him as a visionary who made the first efforts to bring Arabs and Israelis together. Arabs mostly remember him as an appeaser to the United States and Israel, and as a betrayer of Arab interests. The fact that Sadat and Begin won the Nobel Peace Prize in 1978 did not change their view of his role in history. To many, he was the anti-hero.

In addition, the Egyptian public did not approve of what they perceived as Sadat's domestic policy failures, allowing Western businesses to dominate the Egyptian economy; further, the average citizens were displeased with his family's extravagant lifestyle.

Like many world leaders, Sadat will always carry a mixed legacy, but it is undeniable that his efforts to establish peace were a courageous start, even if they led to a tragic end for the Egyptian president.

The Resources

A television mini-series, *Sadat*, starring Lou Gossett, appeared on U.S. television and is available on video. You can find an analysis of Sadat's political career and policies at *www.arab.net*.

Books about Sadat include *Anwar al-Sadat: In Search of an Identity*, HarperCollins, 1978; *Visionary Who Dared*, Taylor and Francis, 1996; *Anwar Sadat*, Rosen Publishing Group, 2003; and *Anwar Sadat: A Man of Peace*, Children's Press, 1986.

43

Charles Monroe Schulz, *Cartoonist*

Who He Is

How can a man who draws cartoons, and simplistic ones at that, be one of our heroes? The reason is quite simple: He both made us laugh out loud and had a keen insight into human behavior, especially our foibles.

Charles Schulz communicated to the world through a protagonist who just could not win, a dog who wanted to be an aviator, a sometimes mean-spirited girl, a boy who dragged a blanket around and a bunch of birds that lived their lives on top of a dog house. Anything unusual about all of this? Seemingly not. His humor was insightful, cute, at times mean and frustrating, but always ultimately warm and supportive.

Yes, Charles Schulz was a genius, a rich man (who refused to allow the comic strip to be written by anyone else) and a daily feature of our lives. But just as importantly, he knew our nature and took a great deal of pleasure in poking fun at us through his characters. And we adored him for it!

What Made the Man

Schulz was born on November 26, 1922, in Minneapolis, Minnesota, to Dena and Carl Schulz. He actually grew up in St. Paul. From an early age, Schulz might have been destined to be a cartoonist: He got the nickname Sparky from one of his uncles, Sparky being a character in the then-popular *Barney Google* comic strip. The name stuck; Schulz would be called Sparky by family and friends for the rest of his life.

He was a good student and skipped two half-grades in elementary school. This might have worked against him when he entered high school, where he was the youngest student attending Central High. Schulz became more and more shy and had few friends. He kept himself entertained by taking correspondence courses from the Art Instruction Inc. school.

He discovered he had a knack for cartooning.

Any thoughts at that age of pursuing art were put on hold when Schulz was drafted into the U.S. Army in 1943 (shortly after his mother died). After training at Camp Campbell, he was made an infantry squad leader with the U.S. 20th Armored Division and sent to combat in Europe toward the end of World War II.

After the war was over and Schulz was honorably discharged, he returned to St. Paul and renewed his interest in art as an instructor with Art Instruction, Inc. He decided to see if his work had commercial value. His early drawings were first published by Robert Ripley in *Ripley's Believe It or Not!*, then being published in a Catholic comic book series called *Topix* (the Ripley feature would go on to appear in hundreds of newspapers around the country, but this was after Schulz had stopped submitting further drawings).

By now, Schulz was considering creating a comic strip that would center on the lives of ordinary children. It would not feature cartoon-like, larger-than-life characters or storylines. Instead, it would draw its humor from the struggles of everyday life as seen through the honest eyes of articulate children.

The first version of Schulz's vision was called *Li'l Folks* and ran from 1947 to 1949 in the St. Paul Pioneer Press. The name Charlie Brown was first used in these strips, but the character had not been defined yet. Four different characters were given the name Charlie Brown. Another recurring character in the strip was an unnamed dog that looked very much like an early version of Snoopy.

Schulz approached the Newspaper Enterprise Association in 1948 to have the strip nationally syndicated to other newspapers, but the deal, which would have made Schulz an independent contractor, fell through. The next year, Schulz took his best strips to the powerful United Features Syndicate. United Features liked the work, but changed the name of the strip (for reasons still unknown) to *Peanuts*.

Peanuts made its first appearance in 1950 and immediately started to build up a large fan base. Over the next few years, Schulz would refine the style of the drawing and expand the adult references the characters used. Charlie Brown and Snoopy emerged as the two most prominent characters and were soon joined by equally popular characters: Linus, the blanket-holding philosopher; his crabby sister Lucy; Beethoven-worshipping Schroeder; Pig Pen, who was always surrounded by a cloud of dirt; Charlie's demanding sister Sally; and a bird friend of Snoopy named Woodstock. Later, the strip would add the tomboy Peppermint Patty and her lackey, Marcie.

Schulz started adding running gags to his work. These included Charlie's never-ending failure as a baseball player, his run-ins with a kite-eating tree, his inability to kick a football held by Lucy, Lucy's establishment of her own sidewalk psychiatry service and Snoopy's obsession with being a World War I flying ace fighting the hated Red Baron.

One of the more interesting, and controversial, aspects of the strip was Schulz's use of religious themes, usually expressed by Linus. Schulz had been active in his church in his early life, but by the 1980s was describing himself as a secular humanist who did not believe in any one theology.

As *Peanuts* thrived and grew, Schulz's personal life went through significant changes. He married Joyce Halverson in 1951 and had five children. They were divorced in 1972 and Schulz married his second wife, Jean Forsyth Clyde, the next year. They would be together until his death.

During this time, Schulz and his family moved briefly to Colorado Springs, returned to Minneapolis and then relocated to Sebastopol, California, where Schulz set up his first real studio. The studio burned down in 1966, and Schulz moved to Santa Rosa, California, where he would work for the rest of his life. While living in Santa Rosa, Schulz maintained an association with hockey and figure skating (both would figure often into Snoopy-themed strips), and became the owner of the Empire Ice Arena in 1969.

During the 1960s and 1970s, *Peanuts* would grow from a popular comic strip into a true pop cultural phenomenon. During this time, Hallmark began the first series of Peanuts-themed greeting cards; the book *Happiness Is a Warm Puppy* appeared on the New York Times' best-seller list; and the strip was featured on the cover of Time magazine. An off-Broadway musical called *You're a Good Man, Charlie Brown* debuted. The strip also has inspired numerous television specials and two feature films. Snoopy's battle with the Red Baron was made into a top-selling pop record and, in 1969, the Apollo X astronauts named their command module Charlie Brown and the Lunar Excursion Module Snoopy.

Mostly on his own, Schulz worked on the *Peanuts* strip uninterrupted for almost 50 years. The work came to a stop in 1999 when Schulz suffered a stroke. Doctors later discovered he had colon cancer that had metastasized to his stomach. Chemotherapy side effects restricted his vision and he announced his retirement later that year at the age of 77. Schulz died of a heart attack on February 12, 2000. The last original strip ran the next day.

The Legacy of the Man

Charles Schulz redefined how humor could be expressed in comic strips, and firmly believed that wisdom could come from the mouths of babes. The public responded to this and made the strip a tremendous success. Schulz received two Reuben Awards for his cartooning; won a Peabody Award for one of his television specials; was honored with a star on the Hollywood Walk of Fame (next to Walt Disney's); and was posthumously awarded the Congressional Gold Medal, the highest honor the U.S. Congress can give a civilian.

Schulz was saddened by his inability to continue his strip, telling people that "it was taken away from him." He wanted the strip to end when he died and was adamant about no new strips being drawn by someone else. However, older strips are still appearing in newspapers and Schulz's estate continues to earn substantially from the merchandising of the characters. Not long ago, Forbes magazine called Schulz the highest-paid deceased person in America.

The Resources

The television specials and films based on *Peanuts* are available on DVD and video. Compilations of his strips are still some of the most popular books being sold. You can learn more about Schulz and his creations at *www.unitedmedia. com/comics/peanuts*.

Books on the life and art of Charles Schulz include *Charles M. Schulz: Cartoonist and Creator of Peanuts*, Enslow Publishing, 2002; *Charles M. Schulz: Conversations*, University Press of Mississippi, 2002; and *Good Grief: The Story of Charles M. Schulz*, McMeel Publishing, 2005.

Frank Sinatra, *Entertainer*

Who He Is

Why is Frank Sinatra one of our modern heroes? Because he could sing and entertain us like no one else. Four generations of music and movie fans have placed Frank Sinatra on the top of their hit parade. No matter what music is in style, Sinatra is always in style. In recent years, his mellow voice and famous lyrics have been the background to some of the classiest parties and best restaurants and watering holes worldwide. There is not a single country where his songs are not played and where his reputation as a singer and entertainer is not exalted.

His career spanned seven decades and, with few exceptions, his style was bigger than life–literally above the crowd and almost untouchable. He was not an innocent hero; nor was he known for his great charitable works. He ate, drank, smoked and partied his way through life–married a number of times and was part of the famous Rat Pack. He associated with politicians and gangsters, and not necessarily in that order.

He is our hero because he made us feel good (or sad or blue) in song, through movies and in his life. He was blue-collar, brash and absolutely a man of the world. And we loved him for it all.

What Made the Man

Francis Albert Sinatra was born on December 12, 1915, in Hoboken, New Jersey–a classic blue-collar town, though his family was solidly middle class. His first musical break came when he appeared with his group, The Hoboken Four, on *Major Bowes Amateur Hour*. The group won top honors and Frank's career was begun, including a stint as a singing waiter–can you imagine Old Blue Eyes delivering the main course with a song?

His first national break came with a stint with the famous bandleader Harry James, and then with the even more popular bandleader, Tommy Dorsey. (The famous scene in *The Godfather*–"I'll make him an offer he can't refuse"–is a vague reference to Sinatra's getting out of a contract with a bandleader to pursue his own, individual career.) The 1940s were the beginning of a tremendous decade-long success story–particularly with teenage girls–again *The Godfather*, when the Sinatra-like character comes to entertain the bride and groom, and the young girls swoon.

Sinatra, like all other eligible young men, tried to join the war by volunteering, only to be turned down for health reasons. This made him free to pursue his career, which he did with a passion, including his first appearance in the movies. His popularity and his music were unmatched through the early 1950s. But tastes change, as they always do. So, too, did Sinatra's career. The young people were interested in other singers and other music. It was the movie *From Here to Eternity* that not only saved his career, but launched it to new heights. This was followed closely by his portrayal of a would-be presidential killer (*Suddenly*) and a heroin addict (*The Man With the Golden Arm*).

So what had been a slight pause turned into full-blown success as his movie exposure revitalized his singing career–so much so that he had his own label, Reprise Records, with Capital in the early 1960s. It was in this unique role that the famous moniker, Chairman of the Board was born. For whatever reason, Capital refused to renew his contract, making perhaps one of the biggest blunders in recording history. Be that as it may, there was no limit for this popular, rough-edged star and singer.

Next stop, Las Vegas and continued fame and fortune!

By the early 1950s, Las Vegas had become one of the most famous and outrageous places in America. Famed for gambling, prostitution and gangsters, it also was the live entertainment capital of the world. Sinatra and his cronies, affectionately referred to as the Rat Pack, were a huge part of the Vegas scene and an immediate hit with crowds who swarmed to see and hear Frank Sinatra–along with Dean Martin, Sammy Davis Jr., Peter Lawford, Joey Bishop and sometimes Shirley MacLaine.

Sinatra and his Rat Pack became institutionalized when, in 1960, the movie *Ocean's Eleven* was released. Naturally, the movie was about highly-talented, clever thieves whose intent was to rob Las Vegas casinos–something which had never been done before. The fantastic on-screen personalities, combined with a great storyline and script, made the movie and its actors a huge success and simply furthered the public's adoration for and fascination with Sinatra and his friends and playmates.

Of course, the Vegas lifestyle and his movie career were not terribly compatible with a stable home life. Frank was not particularly faithful. Enter wife number two: actress Ava Gardner, whom he married in 1951 and subsequently divorced in 1957. Wife number three was Mia Farrow, in 1968. She was substantially younger than Sinatra; not surprisingly, that marriage ended 2 years after it had begun. Finally, wife number four enters the picture in 1976; her name was Barbara Max and she would be Frank's wife until he died.

A very strange episode in Sinatra's life took place in 1963 when his son, Frank Jr., was kidnapped. A ransom was paid and his son was returned safely. The kidnappers were eventually caught and punished. A story circulated around this time that Sinatra started carrying around a roll of dimes because the kidnappers would talk to him only on public pay phones. Even after the kidnapping was resolved, Sinatra continued to carry the roll of dimes around with him—it became a lifelong habit. (In fact, he was buried with a roll of dimes in his pocket!)

He continued to perform and wow audiences almost up to his death. In the 1990s he recorded the *Duets* album with U2's Bono (see Chapter 7).

The Legacy of the Man

How does the world look upon the life and work of Frank Sinatra? It is hard to imagine any performer who was able to retain his popularity for so long, even at a time when he seemed to be in decline. He managed two or three times to reinvent himself through his music, movies and Las Vegas performances. He has created a library of music so popular, so classic in its tone, that almost every generation to come will listen to Sinatra music in some form during their lives.

Naturally, he is a complicated man—a man of the world. A very interesting subtext in his life was his association with the Kennedy family on one side and his relationship with Sam Giancana and the Mafia on the other. (In fact the sometimes remote, sometimes direct relationship between John Kennedy and Sam Giancana itself has filled volumes of fact and speculations, with Sinatra smack in the middle of it all.)

There is no doubt that if there is such a thing as guilt by association, Sinatra would have been tried and convicted. His whole life was influenced by friendships with Giancana and Lucky Luciano, and his association with Mafia types in Chicago, Miami and Bergen County, New Jersey. He lost (and subsequently regained) his gaming license in Nevada and was frequently investigated by the FBI. The standing joke was that he was the most investigated entertainer in the country.

While he hated the publicity and the accusations, including several unauthorized biographies, he made no bones about the fact that where he grew up (during Prohibition and in New Jersey) there were illegal saloons run by gangsters. If you wanted to work–as a singer–you had to associate with gangsters. He insisted to his dying day that he was not and was never a part of the Mafia.

In any case, throughout his life, his personal comings and goings–marriages, children, lifestyle, known associates–filled newspapers and magazines with speculation, fact, fiction and nonsense. He not only survived this chaos, he thrived in its midst. And to his credit, he was absolutely opposed to segregation and the treatment of his friend Sammy Davis Jr. He used his power to work against such discrimination.

The Resources

Two interesting Websites to visit, among others, are *www.franksinatra.com and www.franksinatrafoundation.com*.

Books on Sinatra include *Sinatra: The Life*, Knopf, 2005; *The Way You Wear Your Hat: Frank Sinatra and the Lost Art of Livin'*, Harper Paperbacks, 1999; *His Way: The Unauthorized Biography of Frank Sinatra*, Bantam, 1987; and *Frank Sinatra: An American Legend*, Reader's Digest, 1998.

Superman,
Comic Strip Hero

Who He Is

Can Superman really be our hero? Absolutely. In fact, he has been a hero for generations, and with a movie that came out in 2006 (with others to follow, no doubt), his reputation as an invincible doer of good deeds will live on. Superman, of course, is merely one of a pantheon of comic book heroes.

The creators of our comic book heroes knew what every good fiction writer knows: The imagination can create characteristics and events that are far more powerful and entertaining than anything that reality has to offer. In Superman, the writers and illustrators created a hero who can never be ruined by bad press, go out of style or fail in an act of heroism.

What Made the Man

Superman is arguably the most famous comic book superhero, with a 70-year history that has moved the character through countless battles and relationships with supervillains, friends and family.

Superman was created by a Canadian artist, Joe Shuster, and an American writer, Jerry Siegel, in 1932. Superman was one of the first major characters for what was known at the time as Detective Comics (now DC Comics) in a series called Action Comics. The character was an immediate hit and became DC's franchise persona, following success in the comic books with stage, movie and television appearances.

Over the years, the history of Superman has evolved, but the basics remain the same. Superman is actually an alien named Kal-El, born on the planet Krypton to renowned scientist Jor-El and his wife, Lara. When Jor-El realizes that Krypton is going to be destroyed, he places his infant son in an intergalactic spaceship and sends him to Earth (for reasons that are still being debated).

His Kryptonian parents realize that Kal-El will have abilities beyond any that normal Earth people possess, including the ability to fly, invulnerability to injury, X-ray and heat vision, and incredible strength. However, the child does not know this—yet. Kal-El's spaceship crashes on Earth in rural farm country near the town of Smallville. He is rescued from the ship by an older Earth couple, John and Martha Kent.

The Kents raise the boy as a normal human named Clark, and as he grows into his teens he discovers some of his superpowers. After the death of his adopted parents, Clark travels to the far north and uses Kryptonian technology to build the Fortress of Solitude, which will be Superman's headquarters. There he finally learns who he is and why he was sent to Earth. He decides to use his powers to fight for truth, justice and the American Way, and moves to the large city of Metropolis.

Clark Kent goes to work as a reporter for the Daily Planet (originally called the Daily Star), which gives him the opportunity to find out about any threats to humanity. He makes friends with fellow reporter Lois Lane (a friendship that will develop into a love affair), cub reporter and photographer Jimmy Olsen and the newspaper's acerbic editor, Perry White. He is now poised to be the savior of mankind.

Superman became a franchise whose demands the original creators could not meet. Although Shuster's and Siegel's bylines stayed with the comics for many years, other artists and writers slowly began to take over the series and flesh out Superman's backstory and add to his abilities.

As the character developed, the writers began using a variety of villains and alternative universes (such as the Bizaro World) to challenge him. Superman was vulnerable to various forms of Kryptonite (fragments of his exploded home planet), but the writers decided the character's amazing abilities were limiting their ability to create compelling stories around him (although some writers and fans embraced the concept of Superman's omnipotence).

Because of this, Superman's invulnerability and strength were reduced to increase the possibility that the character could be defeated. This culminated in the breathtaking decision to have Superman killed by a villain appropriately named Doomsday. Superman was resurrected as a darker figure, although the supporting characters and story settings remained basically the same.

Throughout his life, one of the major challenges to Clark Kent was keeping his Superman identity a secret, so that his enemies could not use his friends against him. The writers, over the years, came up with some innovative ideas, including having Superman possess the ability to hypnotize his friends to mask his identity and to physically change his appearance as Clark Kent.

Other characters became essential to the Superman universe as both villains and allies. The most famous of them are the evil genius Lex Luthor, childhood sweetheart Lana Lang, Supergirl (a cousin of Superman from Krypton), the younger Superman character known as Superboy and perhaps the strangest in Krypto, a superdog companion. Superman also became a member of the Justice League of America, which united him with other superheroes such as Wonder Woman, Green Lantern and Aquaman.

Despite all the changes, one thing remained certain: The world knew that when danger threatened, they could look up and say: "It's a bird, it's a plane ... no, it's Superman!"

The Legacy of the Man

Superman has been analyzed endlessly as being symbolic of a Christ figure or based on German philosopher Friedrich Nietzsche's concept of the ubermensch. Some fans believe that, since both the Superman creators were Jewish, the character was a version of the Jewish legend of the invincible Golem. One possible influence on the creators of Superman was the pulp fiction character Doc Savage. Savage was never as popular as Superman, but was still a well-loved hero (Savage's nickname is the Man of Bronze). In addition, Superman's joint-creator, Siegel, said he was heavily influenced by the John Carter of Mars and Tarzan stories written by Edgar Rice Burroughs.

Whatever their influence, Superman's creators came up with something that has touched people's imaginations for decades. Life was not so great for the creators themselves, who had a troubled relationship with their publishers and had to go to court to get a fair share of the huge profits generated by their creation. Thanks to their efforts and the passion of their fans, any use of the name Superman in any version has to include the citation that he was created by Jerry Siegel and Joe Shuster.

Superman, of course, became much more than just a comic book figure. He is one of those rare fictional characters that have succeeded in a variety of different media. Among them are cartoons by the Max Fleischer studios (there have been many other animated versions of Superman and the Justice League of America), a 1940s movie serial starring Kirk Alyn, the popular 1950s television series starring George Reeve, and a Broadway musical. The character has remained in the public eye through four film appearances by Christopher Reeve, the television series *Lois and Clark* starring Dean Cain and Terri Hatcher and *Smallville*, the early story of Superman, starring Tom Welling. The Superman story was brought back to the big screen in *Superman Returns*, directed by Bryan Singer and starring Brandon Routh.

Superman has also made his way into pop songs and other references. Comedian Jerry Seinfeld used his passion for the character as a plot point for his television series, and appeared in a commercial with an animated Man of Steel (voiced by Patrick Warburton, who also appeared in Seinfeld's television show as David Puddy). Basketball star Shaquille O'Neal has the Superman symbol tattooed on his arm.

Classical music has been touched by Superman, who appears in composer Michael Daugherty's *Metropolis Symphony*. A small town in downstate Illinois renamed itself Metropolis and holds an annual Superman festival.

There seems to be no end to what Superman can do.

The Resources

Almost all of the animated series, movies and television shows starring Superman and the related characters are available on DVD or videocassette. The Superman comic books are still published by DC, and the Man of Steel has been portrayed in other graphic novels. Early versions of the Superman comics are highly sought-after collector items. There are numerous fan Websites devoted to Superman, including *www.supermanhomepage.com* and *www.supermansupersite.com*

Books, besides the comics and graphic novels, about Superman include *Superman: The Ultimate Guide to the Man of Steel*, DK Children, 2006; *The Science of Superman*, ibooks, 2005; *Superman: The Complete History*, Chronicle Books, 2004; and *Greatest Superman Stories Ever Told*, DC Comics, 1986.

46

Mother Teresa,
Missionary

Who She Is

Mother Teresa is surely one of the most famous names of the last 50 years, having garnered almost every honor and award for her tireless work with the homeless and poor in India. So great is her personal and spiritual renown that the Roman Catholic Church began the process of beatification almost immediately upon her death—in fact, she is now Blessed Teresa of Calcutta—and ultimately she may be canonized as a saint of the church.

Is it possible for someone who has done so much good—who has received the Nobel Peace Prize and who is beatified by her church—to be controversial? Perhaps it is the fate of all great heroes to be controversial in some way. In the case of Mother Teresa, some—including more liberal Catholics—consider her views and interpretations of doctrine and Catholic practice far too conservative and strict. She was absolutely and fundamentally against abortion and contraception, and equally vocal on the immorality of divorce.

The confidante of popes and presidents, she was awarded a state funeral in India upon her death. But it was her life, not her death, that continues to motivate and inspire men and women of good will to care for the homeless, children with HIV and victims everywhere.

What Made the Woman

Mother Teresa has so long been associated with India that many forget that she was actually born in what is now part of modern Macedonia, of Albanian parents in 1910. (The modern states of Macedonia and Albania did not exist at the time, as a good part of that area was still part of the former Ottoman Empire.) From an early age, she was active in Catholic youth groups and showed interest in working in the missions. By age 17, she had joined the Sisters of Loretto, an Irish order of sisters, and eventually was assigned to Calcutta as a teacher of geography and catechism at St. Mary's High School. In 1944, she became the principal of St. Mary's. Soon, Sister Teresa contracted tuberculosis, was unable to continue teaching and was sent to Darjeeling for rest and recuperation. It was on the train to Darjeeling that she received her second calling.

Mother Teresa recalled later: *"I was to leave the convent and work with the poor, living among them. It was an order. I knew where I belonged, but I did not know how to get there."*

In 1948, the Vatican granted Sister Teresa permission to leave the Sisters of Loretto and pursue her calling under the jurisdiction of the Archbishop of Calcutta. Mother Teresa started with a school in the slums to teach the children of the poor. She also learned basic medicine and went into the homes of the sick to treat them. In 1949, some of her former pupils joined her. They found men, women and children dying on the streets, rejected by local hospitals. The group rented a room so they could care for helpless people otherwise condemned to die in the gutter. In 1950, the group was established by the church as a Diocesan Congregation of the Calcutta Diocese. It was known as the Missionaries of Charity.

What is most extraordinary is the sheer momentum of her movement within the church. She began with 12 followers, members of her religious order, and the organization grew to some 4,000 plus a related group of religious men. In addition, tens of thousands gathered around the Missionaries of Charity as a huge support group, both active in the ministry as well as helping to secure donations and financing in order to fund the work.

There was not a group of downtrodden individuals that the Missionaries and Mother Teresa did not try to help. Much of her early work focused on the homeless and dying of Calcutta, especially those of the so-called untouchable class. But not satisfied with that, she helped lepers, AIDS victims, refugees, the handicapped, orphans, victims of natural disasters and just about anyone who needed help. By 1965, Mother Teresa was granted permission to expand her ministry outside of India, to other parts of Asia, Africa and South America, and even the Bronx in New York City. At the end of the 20th century, more than 500 missions, hospices, orphanages and other institutions were founded and operating for the benefit of millions. It is estimated by one source that nearly one million workers are employed by the Missionaries of Charity for charitable work.

What is extraordinary is that her work attracted so many women and men to a life in a religious community, when orders of nuns, brothers and priests throughout the world have been in precipitous decline for decades. As her fame increased, so, too, did the accolades heaped upon her–including the Nobel Peace Prize and the Presidential Medal of Freedom. Such honors had little effect on her work or her views of the world and the church she served. She refused to compromise in her beliefs.

After suffering deteriorating health for a number of years, she died in September of 1997 just after her 87th birthday. Almost immediately, the process for beatification and canonization began.

The Legacy of the Woman

How should we understand this woman and her views of the world and beyond? By any measure, Mother Teresa has fascinated the world by being a complete and utter contrarian. No modern-day view of the church and its mission for her; rather, a strong, simplistic approach to charity and to religious works. Her heroism is based on the belief of the dignity of the individual, no matter how poor, how sick or how low on the social pecking order he or she may be.

But there are critics. Some now believe that she misrepresented the goals of her efforts, and that the money she received was not used for hospitals and hospices, but rather for pure missionary work–converting people to Catholicism. One individual went public with his comments, so strikingly against Mother Teresa and her order as to call them a cult; instead of helping people out of poverty, some claim she believed that being poor was almost a blessing from God.

One controversial practice, common in the Catholic Church, was to baptize the dying–the notion being that once baptized they have an opportunity to be with God. The problem is that many people felt that Mother Teresa and her followers had no right to make that decision, especially in societies like India that are not primarily Christian. Also, there were some who criticized the quality of health care being provided at the various clinics run by the sisters.

Whether the specific criticisms leveled against Mother Teresa or her order are true or not, most people view Mother Teresa as a woman who profoundly influenced not only the Catholic Church but also society at large. The work she began continues today; her influence is and will remain strong as long as the Missionaries of Charity continues its good works on behalf of the poor and sick. While not everyone can and will agree with the particulars of her activities and programs, she remains far and away the most admired individual of the late 20th century. Her life, teachings and good works represent a call to all of us to come to the aid of those neglected by the world or simply ignored and forgotten. She is and will remain a hero with unparalleled personal and spiritual appeal.

The Resources

For more information about efforts to canonize Mother Teresa, visit *www. motherteresacause.info.*

To learn about Mother Teresa's Nobel Prize in Peace visit: www.nobelprizes. com/nobel/peace/1979a.html

Desmond Mpilo Tutu,
Bishop

Who He Is

Many would consider religion and politics a volatile mixture, one that almost never works. One ends up corrupting the other. But Desmond Tutu is our hero because he is truly one of the outstanding exceptions to this rule. He used neither his religious nor his political influence to impose an orthodoxy on the rest of South Africa.

Rather, he made his pulpit a conscience for the nation and the world. He used his religious position to make men and women free and able to live in their own country without the hated apartheid system. He used his prestige not for his own benefit, but to remind the world that so much injustice must not be ignored.

What Made the Man

The Most Reverend Desmond Tutu was the first black South African Anglican Archbishop of Cape Town. He used his position as a cleric to be a diligent fighter of his country's repressive apartheid policies, and to promote the ascension of the African National Congress and Nelson Mandela to national power. Tutu is credited with creating the term Rainbow Nation for the new and inclusive system.

Tutu was born in Klerksdorp, Transvaal, on October 7, 1931. He moved to Johannesburg with his family when he was 12. His father was a teacher and, after Tutu realized his family could not afford to send him to medical school (to follow his dream of being a physician), he decided to take up his father's career and also become a teacher.

He attended the Pretoria Bantu Normal College and eventually graduated from the University of South Africa in 1954. He taught briefly at the Johannesburg Bantu Education School until 1957 when he resigned after the passage of the Bantu Education Act. Tutu believed this act would severely limit the educational prospects of black South Africans.

However, this act was only one part of the far-reaching system of legalized segregation known as apartheid. The National Party had risen to power in the mid 20th century promising to create and maintain apartheid. The races were divided and segregated into specific living areas. Only white South Africans could vote in national elections. Interracial marriage was prohibited and blacks were barred from certain jobs or organizing labor unions. Blacks required passports even to travel within their own country.

Tutu became more and more politicized during this establishment of apartheid and sought a way to help his repressed people. His bishop encouraged Tutu to study for the Anglican priesthood and Tutu was ordained a priest in 1960. At the same time, the government further expanded apartheid by instituting the forced relocation of blacks from newly designated white areas. Millions of black South Africans were moved to the homelands and permitted to return only as officially designated guest workers.

By now, Tutu was the chaplain of the University of Fort Hare, one of the few good colleges for blacks and a center of protest against apartheid. Tutu decided to pursue his studies out of the country and attended King's College in London from 1962 until 1966, receiving a master's degree in theology. He returned to South Africa in 1967 and taught theology for the next 5 years before returning to England to serve as an assistant director of the World Council of Churches. In 1975, Tutu came back to South Africa as the first black to serve as dean of St. Mary's Cathedral in Johannesburg. He served from 1975 to 1978 as the bishop of Lesotho. Finally, in 1978, Tutu was named the first black general secretary of the South African Council of Churches.

Tutu immediately used his new position to denounce apartheid, calling for equal rights for all South Africans. He promoted nonviolent opposition to the white government and the use of economic boycotts. The government responded by revoking his passport, but international protest led to his privileges being restored.

In 1984, Tutu was awarded the Nobel Peace Prize not only as a gesture to his efforts but as an acknowledgement of the oppression of black South Africans. Two years later, he was elected archbishop of Cape Town.

He was the first black to be archbishop, which essentially made him the head of the Anglican Church in South Africa.

By the late 1980s domestic and international pressure (including sanctions) against the white government of South Africa led to the release of Nelson Mandela and the gradual repeal of the apartheid laws. Finally, in 1994, national elections were held in which both blacks and whites could vote. The African National Congress easily won power and Nelson Mandela was made the first black president of a multiracial South Africa.

One of Mandela's first appointments after gaining power was to make Tutu the chair of the newly created Truth and Reconciliation Commission. The commission was charged with investigating human rights violations under the apartheid government of the past 34 years. Tutu was chosen for this important position because of his advocacy of forgiveness and cooperation—rather than promoting acts of revenge for past injustices.

Tutu retired as the archbishop of the Anglican Church in 1996, but maintained his political activism. He was named archbishop emeritus and is now a professor of theology at Emory University in Atlanta, Georgia.

The Legacy of the Man

Desmond Tutu will be remembered as a brave activist against a corrupt system and as a proponent of change without violence, making forgiveness and reconciliation the primary way to effect political change. While he may have retired from the church, he has maintained his interest in social causes both in his native country and around the world.

He criticized the government of Robert Mugabe in Zimbabwe, famously commenting that it appeared that Mugabe "has lost his mind." He expressed support for the West Papuan Independence Movement, criticizing the United Nations for helping Indonesia take over the area.

One of Tutu's more controversial stances was his stated belief that the Israeli treatment of native Palestinians was a form of apartheid. These views were widely criticized by Israel and its supporters, but led to Tutu, in 2003, being made a patron of the Palestinian Christian Sabeel Ecumenical Liberation Theology Center in Jerusalem.

He has supported toleration of homosexuals and has advocated the use of condoms to help fight the rapid spread of HIV/AIDS in South Africa. He was dismayed when Cardinal Joseph Ratzinger was made Pope Benedict XVI, believing the new pope would do little to promote condom use to fight sexually transmitted diseases.

Tutu was an outspoken critic of President George W. Bush's decision to invade Iraq as part of the global war on terror. He called the act mind-boggling and was appalled that the British government of Tony Blair would support the invasion. As part of this protest, he criticized imprisoning suspected terrorists without trial in Guantanamo Bay, Cuba.

Besides the Nobel Peace Prize, Tutu has been honored by receiving Marymount University's 2004 Ethics Award and the Sydney Peace Prize and by giving the commemoration oration as part of the King's College's 175th anniversary (the students' union nightclub is named Tutu's in his honor).

Perhaps Tutu's life and work were best described by Nelson Mandela when he said: "Sometimes strident, often tender, never afraid and seldom without humor, Desmond Tutu's voice will always be the voice of the voiceless."

Tutu may best be remembered by his soft-spoken logical approach to the problems of his country. He often used humor to defuse angry feelings and was an ardent supporter of nonviolent protest (even when Mandela had crossed over to use violence to protest apartheid). His work before apartheid and as part of the historic Truth and Reconciliation Commission set a tone for forgiveness and co-existence that many South Africans hope will be a blueprint to a new and vital future.

The Resources

Desmond Tutu makes an appearance in the anti-violence film *Peace Jam*, available on DVD. There is more information about him and his current efforts through the Desmond Tutu Peace Foundation at *www.tutu.org*.

Books by and about Tutu and the anti-apartheid movement include *No Future Without Forgiveness*, Image, 2000; *God Has a Dream: A Vision of Hope for Our Time*, Doubleday, 2004; *The Rainbow People of God*, Image, 1996; *Rabble-Rouser for Peace: The Authorized Biography of Desmond Tutu*, Free Press, 2006; *The Wisdom of Desmond Tutu*, Westminster John Knox Press, 2000; and *Desmond Tutu: Bishop of Peace*, Children's Press, 1986.

Oprah Winfrey, *Entertainer*

Who She Is

If there is an archetypal rags-to-riches story, one that has inspired millions of adoring fans, it belongs to Oprah (as she is affectionately called). She has become one of the richest women in American, frequently showing up on Fortune's list of the wealthy. She has hosted a television show that is a must for millions of people, founded a production company, starred in full-length movies and is a mover and shaker for writers who dream of being included in her book club. A mere mention by Oprah through any of her media holdings assures prominence and instant fame.

Yet at the same time, there is an enduring quality about this woman who goes to great efforts to expose the hardships and problems within society–particularly those that affect women. (It does not hurt that the controversial subjects help television ratings!)

She is highly admired, consistently appearing on lists of the most popular as well as the most respected. She has been on the cover of Time magazine and enjoys the confidence of dozens of well-respected politicians, entertainers and businesspeople.

What Made the Woman

Oprah Gail Winfrey was born in 1954 in Kosciusko, Mississippi, to barely working-class parents. Most people who have watched her television show know that she had a very difficult childhood, having spent time with her mother, grandmother and her father–some of whom were supportive, some not. Her grandmother taught her to read at a very early age and was very helpful to the small child. At some point, the decision was made to send Oprah to Milwaukee to live with her mother, who seemingly was less supportive and less concerned about the child and her development.

Despite her lackluster family life, Oprah channeled her energies into getting good grades. While in high school, she is reported to have rebelled against her mother, and was sent to Nashville to live with her father, who was stricter but also more encouraging. Education, again, was a priority and she earned honors in high school. She joined the high school speech team and won a national oratory contest, which was instrumental in her advancing her education at Tennessee State University, one of the fine historically black colleges.

To no one's surprise, the outgoing co-ed majored in communications and had her start in the broadcast industry at just 17 years of age working at a local radio station. This experience and her degree from Tennessee State helped her land her first television job in Nashville as a news anchor. Her career moved right along– next to Baltimore as a news anchor and a co-host for a talk show, called *People Are Talking*. (This move, of course, set the stage for the future *Oprah Winfrey Show* from Chicago!)

The move to Chicago to host a very mediocre talk show, AM Chicago, was a real challenge for both her and the station. To this day, Winfrey regards the risk taken by the producer at WLS-TV in Chicago as the great moment in her life. Simply stated, it was not good business to hire a slightly overweight black woman to host a talk show. Further, she was competing with the very popular and established Phil Donahue, who had the highest rankings in daytime talk at the time.

Not only did she succeed in raising the ratings for AM Chicago, but it was expanded to a full hour and renamed *The Oprah Winfrey Show*–and she never looked back from there. With national syndication in 1986, the show topped all others of its kind, hit new records in viewership and became the standard against which all other similar shows were judged.

As the show progressed over the years, its standards changed. Initially, like all daytime talk shows, sensation was the norm. Certainly, Winfrey had to compete with Donahue and others on the same level; she was not a name, and was not famous as a reporter or interviewer. However, her show also took on more serious, rather than only sensational, issues. She addressed what was important to women in particular, but also society in general. Health and welfare were as much a part of the show as entertainers.

Her book club paved the road to success (the Oprah effect) for any individual whose work fascinated or interested her. A recent episode concerned an author who had plagiarized parts of a best-selling novel, to the extreme embarrassment of the host. One author is reported to have said that he did not want to be part of the book club, an amazing statement from someone who was about to reap the benefit of one of the greatest marketing machines ever conceived. He later changed his mind. However, once rejected, there was no way to redeem his status or position; Winfrey certainly did not need him.

Our hero is more than just a talk show host. She is an actress, businesswoman and studio mogul, publisher, station owner and all-around financial success. Her various endeavors have produced a net worth estimated to be over $1.4 billion in assets—though who really knows for sure? Her Harpo studios on the west side of Chicago (not as poor as it once was) represent her major achievement, though she can claim dozens of other great successes, not least her performance in *The Color Purple.*

Because she changed the format of her show to a less controversial and confrontational, more reasoned and thoughtful style, she increasingly became the spokesperson on many issues that involved those not in the mainstream: gays, lesbians, AIDS, fate of women in the Third World and more. Her middle-aged audience responded well to such changes and seems to mirror her own personal interests and charitable concerns.

The Legacy of the Woman

Oprah is our hero because she is, and will continue to be, successful in spite of poverty and a less-than-stable upbringing. She is our hero because she is willing to take risks, to bring people on the show in order to raise consciousness about events and forces that might not be controllable, but which at least need to be understood.

Those who have worked for her know that she is a tough taskmaster—but most great businesspeople do not get to the top being shy or laid back. And there is a puzzling part of her personality that just cannot shake her physical image: much of her personal effort over the years has revolved around her obsession with her weight and general wellness.

> Most would agree that better nutrition and health
> are great ideas, but her yo-yo diets and constant
> preoccupation about her weight have been a distraction
> for her audience and distracted from her message.

She is our hero because she is not afraid to use her money to further causes that she believes in. Personal contributions, other than the millions raised through her show and various benefits, are said to be some of the highest as a percentage of wealth of any contemporary philanthropists. She created the Angel Network, a feature on her show, which showcases individuals who work in obscurity to serve the most needy and underprivileged. Her direct support, plus the publicity garnered from the appearance on television, ensures that these special angels receive immediate financial assistance to further their charitable works.

Oprah Winfrey certainly is not the typical television personality and entertainer. She is complicated, outspoken, liberal (but not always), a believer in personal responsibility, rich, influential, strong-willed, insightful, popular and strangely aloof. She seemingly has an endless appetite for new projects, media and otherwise, shows no interest in winding down the television show (although she has threatened several times to quit TV on a regular basis) and seems highly motivated to make a personal and professional difference in the world.

Oprah is our hero because she has made, and continues to make, a difference in the way we think and feel about our world, about the people with whom we interact and about ourselves. She is our hero because she expects the best from us, no matter our circumstances and background. And she is our hero because throughout it all, she is forever the entertainer. The stage is hers.

The Resources

Oprah has co-authored a number of books. Visit *www.amazon.com* or other online resellers. The most recent of these books was published in 1999.

Tiger Woods,
Athlete

Who He Is

He is our hero not just for his good looks, personable public image and incredible skill as a golfer, but also because he represents a whole new generation of athletes who see his success and are motivated to emulate it in their own sports.

He is our hero because Tiger Woods had one of the most respected amateur careers in the history of golf, and has continued this into his professional career. He is a latter-day version of Arnold Palmer—wildly popular with golfers and nongolfers alike.

What Made the Man

Eldrick (Tiger) Woods was born on December 30, 1975, in Cypress, California. His father, Earl, a retired lieutenant colonel in the U.S. Army, nicknamed him Tiger after a Vietnamese soldier and friend, Vuong Dan Phong. Phong, who had also been given the nickname Tiger by Earl, saved Earl's life during the Vietnam War.

Woods was practically born with a golf ball in one hand and a putter in the other. When he was 6 months old, he reportedly watched his father hit golf balls into a net and imitated his swing. And at age 2, he made an appearance on the *Mike Douglas Show*, playing golf with comedian and golfer Bob Hope. He shot 48 for nine holes when he was only 3 years old and featured in Golf Digest when he was 5. He was a six-time Optimist International Junior tournament winner at ages 8-9 and 12-15. However, although golf was important in his family, education always took precedence as Woods was growing up. He attended Western High School in Anaheim, California, where he maintained high grades.

As an amateur, Woods played in the 1992 Nissan Los Angeles Open, which was his first professional tournament. He was only 16 years old. The following year, he competed in three more PGA Tour events and in 1994, he made the 36-hole cut and tied for 34th place in the Johnnie Walker Asian Classic in Thailand, among three other PGA Tour performances. Although he never graduated, Woods started his college career that same year as an economics major at Stanford University in California.

In the 2 years that he played for Stanford, he won 10 collegiate events to clinch the NCAA title at the end of his second season.

By the time he turned professional in late summer of 1996, Woods had won six USGA national championships besides his NCAA victory. He had also won the U.S. Junior Amateur three times and was the first player ever to win that title multiple times. In addition, he was the youngest golfer ever, at age 15, to win the U.S. Junior Amateur and the youngest golfer ever, at age 18, to win the U.S. Amateur, which he would win two more times. When he later swept the U.S. Open, Woods became the first player to obtain all three of the U.S. Open, Amateur and Junior Amateur titles.

The week after he won his third U.S. Amateur title, Woods played his first tournament as a professional. Since he started late in the season, there were only seven events left for him to try and finish among the top 125 money winners and earn a PGA Tour player's card. He did that with a flourish, winning two tournaments and ranking among the top 30 money winners while qualifying for the Tour Championship. Woods finished 25th with $790,594 and was the first rookie since 1990 to win twice and the first player since 1982 to finish in the top five a total of five consecutive times.

In 1997, Woods achieved No. 1 on the Official World Golf Ranking–the most rapid progression ever to that position–and on June 15 of that year, during his 42nd week as a professional golfer, he became the youngest No. 1 golfer in history. He was 21 years, 24 weeks old when he claimed that status, beating out the previous youngest from 1986 by more than 8 years.

Woods won eight times on the PGA Tour in 1999, which was his third full season as a professional and one of his best so far. This made him the first player to win as many as eight PGA Tour events in one season since 1974. That year, he took the PGA Championship and earned $6,616,585, a figure that beat out the previous single-year PGA Tour record. Also in 1999, Woods achieved the highest point average (20.61) in the World Ranking's history, earned a record-setting 750 points and reached the lowest-ever adjusted scoring average (68.43 strokes). He later broke his own record in 2000 by reaching an adjusted scoring average of 67.79 strokes.

Woods' record is astonishing. He won the 1997, 2001, 2002 and 2005 Masters Tournaments, the 1999 and 2000 PGA Championships, the 2000 and 2002 U.S. Open Championships and the 2000 and 2005 British Open Championships. He also became the first major championship winner of African or Asian heritage. Woods holds records for 270 (18 under par) in the Masters, 272 (12 under par) in the U.S. Open and 269 (19 under par) in the British Open. He also shares the PGA Championship record of 270 (18 under par) with Bob May.

Woods is a 5-time PGA Tour money leader and PGA Tour Vardon Trophy winner as well as a 3-time member of the U.S. Presidents Cup team and a 4-time member of the U.S. Ryder Cup team. Here is a list of some of the other awards that he has procured throughout his career as a professional golfer:

- Jack Nicklaus Award, also known as the PGA Tour Player of the Year Award (1997, 1999 to 2003, and 2005)
- Player of the Year Award, PGA of America (1997, 1999 to 2003 and 2005)
- Player of the Year Award, Golf Writers Association of America (1997, 1999 to 2003 and 2005)
- Male Athlete of the Year Award, ESPY (1998–co-winner, 2000 to 2002)
- Sportsman of the Year Award, Sports Illustrated (1996 and 2000)
- World Champion of Champions Award, L'Equipe magazine, France (2000)
- Male Athlete of the Year Award, The Associated Press (1997, 1999 and 2000)
- Sportsman of the Year Award, Reuters (2000)
- World Sportsman of the Year Award, World Sports Academy (1999 and 2000).

The Legacy of the Man

Woods, who married Swedish model Elin Nordegren in October of 2004, not only has a busy professional and personal life, but he also maintains a schedule full of charity work. In 1996, he and his father established the Tiger Woods Foundation, which focuses on projects for children. The foundation's programs include golf clinics aimed at disadvantaged children, a grant program, university scholarships, the Start Something character-building program, an association with Target House at St. Jude Hospital in Memphis, Tennessee, an annual fundraising concert and charity golf tournament, and the Tiger Woods Learning Center. The center is located in Anaheim, California, and opened in February of 2006. Several thousand students are expected to use it each year, taking advantage of its day, after-school, summer, weekend, community outreach and online learning programs.

Besides his own foundation work, Woods has also participated in charity work for his current caddy, Steve Williams. In April of 2006, he won an auto racing event that benefited the Steve Williams Foundation, which raises funds in order to provide sporting careers for underprivileged youth. Together with the editors of *Golf Digest*, Woods has also written a book about golf, *How I Play Golf.*

Woods' father died on May 3, 2006, at the age of 74. He will be missed greatly by Woods, who lost not only his father but his mentor, coach and friend.

After having accomplished so many things in such a short amount of time as a professional golfer, it seems that Woods' career is still on the upswing. As it stands, golf fans everywhere will have his name etched on their brains for a long, long time. And years from now, once he is finished with the sport he loves, Tiger Woods' name will live forever.

The Resources

To read more about the early years of Tiger Woods' life, pick up a copy of *Tiger Woods: The Makings of a Champion*, St. Martin's Paperbacks, 1997.

50

World War II Armed Forces, *Warriors*

Who They Are

They are literally millions of men and women, living or dead, who fought in Europe, Africa and Asia to preserve American freedom and the American way of life. They are the veterans, many still living, who risked everything for a country in need and a world desperate for help to fight and destroy inexpressibly nefarious political systems.

They were ordinary people, most drafted from their daily lives and routines, who were asked to travel overseas, live in miserable and terrifying conditions, and destroy an enemy they had never seen. They did everything that was asked of them, including suffering and dying. And they did it with tremendous heroism. They are the eternal symbols of all members of the armed forces, before and after, who have served their country.

What Made Them

Although hundreds of medals were awarded to deserving service men and women, the real heroes of World War II are ...everybody. Unlike World War I, this was total war, involving a drastic change in the way an entire country conducted its life. And it was a war in which not everyone wanted the United States to become involved.

The rise of Nazi Germany under Adolf Hitler and of the Japanese empire in the 1930s was troubling to the entire world. Most people who had lived through the horrors of World War I believed it to be the war to end all wars. Many peace-loving people hoped that after the devastation of that war and the creation of the League of Nations, the world would never again see a war that caused so many casualties.

The ending of the Great War set the stage for the rise of the Nazis in Germany, the use of the Jewish population as the excuse for Germany's loss and a rise of nationalism that would lead to unprecedented militarism. In 1939, Germany invaded Poland, and France and the United Kingdom quickly declared war. Their armies would be no match for the German method of Blitzkrieg warfare, which emphasized mobility over fixed defenses.

Soon, all of Western Europe, including France, was under control of the Germans. Only the British remained to resist, and suffered heavily from almost constant bombing of military and then civilian targets by the Germans. Meanwhile, the Japanese were quickly taking over much of China and Southeast Asia.

U.S. President Franklin Roosevelt knew that it was only a matter of time before the United States would be involved in the war. He faced heavy opposition from many who believed the United States should not enter what was perceived as a European war. Roosevelt skirted around this issue at first by simply sending needed supplies to the embattled British in a program called Lend-Lease. Then the Japanese attacked the U.S. naval base at Pearl Harbor, Hawaii, without warning on December 7, 1941. Congress quickly declared war and the United States was finally involved in World War II.

However, the U.S. military was in no condition to fight a war. Between World War I and World War II, the United States had cut substantial funding from the military. There were not even enough supplies to train an army. A few professionals had stayed in the armed services, but for the United States to fight the war adequately, it would have to enlist (or draft) citizen soldiers.

The soldiers came from all walks of life. Upper classes fought next to the people who normally would have been working for them. And the armed services comprised ethnicities of all kinds mixed. The U.S. military took a crash course in building up its training capacity, emphasizing physical conditioning in preparation for what would be an exhausting war.

While the so-called democratic army was the pride of the nation, African-Americans were not integrated into the armed forces until after the war–so strong was the prejudice and the hold that segregation had on much of the nation.

Soldiers in the U.S. Army fought mostly in Northern Africa, Italy and finally in Europe. They drove tanks, manned artillery, helped in logistics and administration but, mostly, were foot soldiers known as GIs (for government issue, referring to the clothes that were distributed to everyone). Many of the officers were as inexperienced as the enlisted men. Some of the better soldiers were promoted to command. The Army fought in the heat, rain and snow under grueling conditions, constant fire and having to carry all their supplies on their backs. They eventually marched their way into Berlin and victory.

The U.S. Marines fought primarily in the South Pacific as the United States began a campaign of island-hopping to defeat the Japanese and eventually close in on the home islands. The Marines would be dropped off either on shore or many yards from shore by personnel carriers and would have to wade through water and enemy fire to establish a beachhead. From there, they would slowly move across the island under constant fire from dug-in Japanese troops. The casualties, especially for the Japanese, were staggering.

In the Atlantic, the Navy's main job was to protect the troop and supply convoys moving from the United States to Europe. They had to discover new techniques to defeat the German U-boat fleet of submarines. In the Pacific, the Navy formed into large battle groups revolving around one or more aircraft carriers. The United States also operated most of its submarines in the Pacific, sinking Japanese military and merchant vessels.

Each branch of the service had its own air corps; there would not be a unified Air Force until after the war was over. In Europe, the air corps was used to bomb German targets. In the Pacific, the air missions were mostly to sink Japanese warships and to provide air support to troops battling on the islands.

Two often-neglected parts of the military effort were the Coast Guard and the Merchant Marine. The Coast Guard helped patrol the waters off the U.S. coastlines and also manned the personnel carriers that took Marines into combat in the Pacific. The Merchant Marine was instrumental in keeping the European theater of war supplied and took heavy casualties from German submarines. The Merchant Marine has been referred to as the forgotten arm of the service and finally received an official memorial in 1988.

Women were instrumental in both the services and the home front. Members of the Women's Army Corps (WAC) did not see actual combat but were vital in supporting jobs. A special group of the women's military called the WASPs was responsible for transporting aircraft over the United States to whatever bases they were needed. Women also entered the workplace in unprecedented numbers, helping to create the iconic character of Rosie the Riveter, who symbolized their dedication and hard work.

The average American family also had to undergo hardships to help the war effort. There was rationing of rubber, gasoline, sugar and coffee. Many civilians joined the Civil Defense Corps and helped in air-raid training. Even children learned how to spot aircraft in case they saw an enemy plane in the skies.

The Legacy of the World War II Heroes

The war took a heavy toll, with more than a million Americans killed or wounded. The heroes of World War II both at home and abroad have been referred to as The Greatest Generation. The war has sometimes been called The Good War because of its clear distinction between good and evil.

As is often the case, many veterans suffered debilitating physical and mental problems (now identified as post-traumatic stress syndrome) that would haunt them all their lives. They were often forgotten and neglected, assigned to a series of Veterans Administration hospitals and facilities–in other words, housed for the world never to see again. Despite the problems and heartaches, most Americans during World War II were justly proud of what they did to protect their country and free people from brutal dictatorships.

The Legacy of the World War II Armed Forces

It seems hard to believe, but national monuments to the great or fallen have, in recent years, created quite a bit of controversy-including the Vietnam Veterans Memorial and the World Trade Center Memorial, Reflecting Absence. For reasons that are not always obvious, the design, timing, placement and ultimate construction seem to bring out the worst in people–bitter arguments and fights took place over the National World War II Memorial as well.

If for no other reason, the memorial was a source of consternation because it came about so many years after the war. Local areas, cities and counties had their own memorials, but it seemed odd to many people that the country as a whole did not recognize the gargantuan effort, the tremendous loss of life and general misery, of the World War II veteran. As importantly, their population was aging rapidly and it seemed that nothing would happen in their life-time!

The first effort to get a bill passed in Congress began in 1987, introduced by Ohio Congresswoman Marcy Kaptur. It was not until 1993, with the assistance of Strom Thurmond of South Carolina in the Senate, that a bill finally passed both houses of Congress. The chronology of this effort gets even worse: A Friedrich St. Florian design was chosen by 1997 but work did not begin until 2001. During this time, some $200 million had to be raised to build the design and a location had to be chosen. This site selection process brought on another huge fight; despite protests, it was eventually placed on the National Mall, even though many thought it poorly placed, interrupting the views between the Lincoln Memorial and the Washington Monument.

Begun in late 2001, the memorial took nearly 2½ years to complete. There are 56 pillars representing the then 48 states and various districts and territories, arranged in a semi-circle around a plaza. Two arches, one for the Atlantic and the other for the Pacific, are placed on opposite sides of the plaza. Perhaps most impressive is Freedom Wall, which contains 4,048 gold stars, each representing 100 American deaths which resulted from action in the war. The memorial finally opened to the public in April of 2004, at a time when some 1,000 World War II veterans were dying each day.

Like many activities of this kind, once completed, the memorial has become an accepted part of the Washington landscape and the national consciousness.

The Resources

There are hundreds of documentaries, feature films and television movies on the exploits of Americans at home and abroad during the war. Information on the war can be found at *www.worldwar-2.net*.

There are also hundreds of nonfiction and fiction books on the war. To learn more about how the average American helped fight the war, read *The Greatest Generation*, Random House, 2004; *Citizen Soldiers: The U.S. Army From the Normandy Beaches to the Bulge to the Surrender of Germany*, Simon and Schuster, 1998; and *The Good Fight: How World War II Was Won*, Atheneum, 2001.